Contents

Introduction: SURVIVAL – TEEN ISLAND

SECTION ONE: SCHOOL SURVIVAL

SECTION TWO: COMMUNITY CASTAWAY

SECTION THREE: SOCIAL SMOKE SIGNALS

SECTION FOUR: ISLAND HOME

SECTION FIVE: SERIOUS STUFF

SURVIVAL: TEEN ISLAND
The ultimate survival guide for 15 - 18 year olds.

3

For students and their parents:

This book has been written for young people who are in their senior years of high school. It's a "survival guide" manual with stacks of tips and advice to help minimise the hitches and glitches and maximise access to a fun and fulfilling few years.

By comparing these years to being "stranded" on an island, this book introduces each area in a humorous way, whilst highlighting some of the issues that teenagers face every day. Being on an island is all about survival – sometimes it will be a fun and interesting challenge, other times it can feel quite isolating, and sometimes you might just want to get off altogether!

The sections in this book relate to different areas of the teenager's life:

Section One

School: including tips on tackling homework and exam study;

Section Two

The Community: how to get out there and get a part-time job and handle a new income;

Section Three

Communication: how to relate to others in a mature and impressive way – a skill for life;

Section Four

Home – domestic warfare: how to cope when the parents aren't there!

Section Five

Social Life: drugs, sexuality, relationships, problems, having fun without losing the plot.

The strategies in this book are practical and will hopefully inspire teenagers to become more mature, confident and independent members of their school, community and social world. It doesn't claim to have all the answers (no-one ever does), rather it offers a range of suggestions that can be taken and adapted to suit the individual environment.

Being a teenager isn't always going to be paradise, but it can be a time where you can get out there and explore the big wide ocean of adulthood, and still be within sight of the mainland. Enjoy it while you can!

This book has been reviewed by males and females aged 16 - 18, as well as professionals who work with young people in areas of education, employment and crisis counselling. The publishers wish to thank the following people for their important contributions towards making this book suitable for its audience:

Brendan Ash
Anna Broadhead
Tristen Hindley
Noel Hyland
Anna Laughton
Dr Graham Lawler

Survival:
Teen Island

By Sandy Tasker
Illustrated by Terry Allen
additional material Dr Graham Lawler

Aber publishing

Books to Improve Your Life

Disclaimer

This book is intended as a resource for British adolescents aged 15 – 18. The information included in the book is of a general nature only and is not intended to address the specific situation of any individual. Although comprehensive research has been conducted in the interests of providing quality information, we make no claims, warranties or guarantees about the accuracy or completeness of the content. Individuals experiencing issues covered in this book should seek professional support through their school, parents or qualified professionals; or contact the local/National organisations included as contacts in the book.

Many website addresses and telephone numbers have been included so that specific organisations may be contacted at the reader's discretion. These contact details were correct at the time of publication and may change over time. Similarly, laws and guidelines included in this book may change from time to time and may not represent the most recent information. The information presented does not represent or reflect the opinions of any one organisation and does not constitute legal advice.

If any major changes are brought to our attention, we will attempt to correct them in the subsequent edition. The author/publisher and all/any of their agents are not responsible for the outcomes of actions taken by readers of this book. **Readers and parents of readers are advised to seek professional opinion where necessary and not rely solely on the contents of this book.**

Survival: Teen Island
A resource book for 15 - 18 year olds growing up.

© 2009 Aber Publishing
Printed in Europe

ISBN: 978-1-84285-167-8

Author: Sandy Tasker European Edition edited by Dr Graham Lawler
Cover Design and Layout: Shay Howard
Illustrator: Terry Allen

Acknowledgements:

Photo images used herein were obtained from IMSI's Masterclips/MasterPhotos collection, 1895 Francisco Blvd, East San Rafael, CA 94901-5506 USA, website: **www.imsisoft.com.**

Additional clipart images have been sourced from Corel Corporation, 1600 Carling Ave, Ottawa, Ontario, Canada KIZ8R7.

Published by:

Aber Publishing

P.O. Box 225

Abergele

Conwy County LL18 9AY

U.K.

www.aber-publishing.co.uk

Introduction

Survival-
Teen Island

Welcome to Teen Island

From a distant harbour, you set sail on a ship, journeying out to sea. For the first few years, it's like you hardly even left the bay – the waters are calm, the skies are clear. You don't have to worry about sailing the ship – it is all done for you. This is your childhood, where everything seems simple, your world is small, and other people are in control of your life.

Then, out of the blue, a storm hits. The waves are thundering around you, and everything becomes darkened by the massive black clouds. With the brute force of a bulldozer, you are thrown overboard by a sweeping mass of water. You close your eyes and hang on tightly to a floating piece of debris, thinking that lifejackets are not such a bad fashion statement after all. After what seems like an eternity, you feel solid ground beneath you.

When you open your crusty red eyes and remove the seaweed from your underwear, you find that you are on an island. You cast your eyes along the deserted shores, wondering where on Earth you are, and as if in reply, you look up to see an old, painted sign – "Welcome to Teen Island".

You look around. If this is Teen Island, where is everyone else? Where do you go for food, water and shelter? Is help arriving or are you stuck here forever? As the questions swim around you like sharks, you feel a wave of panic rise up inside you. You stumble along the beach, frantically looking around for signs of civilisation.

Suddenly, you see a bottle, rolling around in the foamy waves. It has something inside it. You walk up and pick up the bottle, pulling out the soaking paper inside. A message is written there:

"You are not alone." What do you mean, I'm not alone, you think? As far as you can see, there is not another soul on the island. You begin to wonder about a bunch of cannibals lurking in the lush island forest. Things are rapidly declining in the luck department. You gaze out to the ocean in the futile hope of a rescue boat coming to whisk you away. No boat. Great! But what you do see is hopeful. In the distance, but still close enough to see, are a bunch of other islands. You instantly know that there are others like you, also stranded in their own adolescence. The message was right. You are not alone. This knowledge calms you enough to collect your thoughts.

You realise that the safe ship of childhood was a happy memory, but you now have to focus on an exciting challenge ahead, Survival. It's not so bad, you think.

You just

have to work out what you need and how you are going to get it – one step at a time. And there are probably some things here that you can find to help you get by. Over the next few days, you find that you are stronger and more resourceful than you ever realised. You manage to make a home, and nourish yourself with food and water. You find a map and get to know your way around the island. It's a bit scary, but the more you look, the more you find. Over time, you find ways of communicating with the other islands. You learn survival tactics from your neighbours. Pretty soon you feel like you are the star of some reality show or Hollywood blockbuster.

One day, you start to build a boat. It's a slow process, making it by hand, but this boat will eventually get you off the island. However, that's years away. For now, you have plenty to do.

This Teen Island can be a fantastic place to stay if you take control and make the most of what you have. There are plenty of things that can make your life easier and more fulfilling, but they won't all appear in front of you like when you were younger.

Finding out how to stand on your own two feet is like an exciting survival mission, one where every success will make you proud and every blunder will simply be a lesson, not the end of the world. So, stuff this survival manual in your pocket (it won't give you all the answers but it will be a good reference) and start making your shabby island into a resort.

'Believe in yourself you do have talent'

Dr Graham Lawler a.k.a. the broadcaster and writer *Mr Educator.*

SURVIVAL: TEEN ISLAND
The ultimate survival guide for 15 - 18 year olds .

7

Survival Checklist

The following is not a test. Use it as a guideline for the things that most teenagers will experience at some stage. Don't worry if you have done some things but not others – everyone is unique and life requires us to do different things at different times.

Place a tick in the boxes where you feel comfortable about the way you are doing things. Place a dot where you have started to think about the area but still have some work to do.

School:

☐ I have a routine for doing my homework that enables me to get everything completed on time.

☐ I have a plan for exam study, which includes compiling information, making study notes and uses at least one revision/memorisation technique.

☐ I have a well-equipped place at home where I can complete my homework and study without distraction.

☐ I have regular breaks for relaxation and/or fitness when I am studying.

☐ I take appropriate notes during lessons and feel comfortable asking for help if I do not understand.

Community:

☐ I feel like I am part of the community in the contributions that I make (e.g. sport, clubs, part-time work).

☐ I have part-time work, which I enjoy, or I have an idea of some part-time work I may wish to do in the future.

☐ I have a resume/CV which I keep up to date.

☐ I have a template for a good cover letter for job applications.

☐ I have experienced job-seeking procedures such as writing letters or attending interviews.

☐ I have at least one good outfit, which I can wear to an interview or another formal occasion.

☐ I have some ideas of the future career I might like to have, and I am seeking experiences that might lead towards this (e.g. work experience, appropriate subjects).

Words and Numbers:

☐ I have a bank account which suits my needs and I know how to make a deposit and withdraw cash.

☐ I keep to a budget which is suitable for my income, and I am able to save a small amount each week towards larger purchases.

More Words and Numbers:

☐ I feel comfortable filling out forms. I have access to details such as my bank account details, emergency contacts, etc.

☐ I feel confident and polite when speaking on the phone to an adult.

☐ I can use maps and timetables to reach most places by car or public transport.

Computer:

I have computer skills which enable me to:

☐ Write a letter or a resume/ C.V..

☐ Send an e-mail.

☐ Search the Internet for research purposes.

☐ Present a school project.

Home:

If I have to fend for myself at home alone for a weekend, I would be able to:

☐ Use a washing machine.

☐ Shop for groceries.

☐ Cook healthy meals for myself.

☐ Clean the house.

☐ Make sure the house is secure at all times.

☐ Locate emergency telephone numbers.

☐ Manage the gardening (e.g. reticulation or sprinkler) and rubbish collection.

Looking After Others:

If left alone with siblings or children that I am babysitting, I am able to:

☐ Entertain them, e.g. games, books, etc.

☐ Ensure that they do not misbehave.

☐ Give the appropriate food.

☐ Get them organised for bathing, dressing and bed, etc.

☐ Handle any accidents or illness.

Self:

☐ I like the person that I am becoming. I know and accept my strengths and limitations.

☐ I am able to express my feelings and needs to others, and I feel happy and safe most of the time.

☐ I have a supportive network of friends and family.

On the next page or on a separate sheet, write some goals down for the areas that you might like to explore and develop over the coming months.

SURVIVAL: TEEN ISLAND
The ultimate survival guide for 15 - 18 year olds .

9

My Goals

Section One:
School Survival

School doesn't have to be a daily endurance challenge. Learn some simple strategies and you'll stay on dry land.

Getting Organised

Life on "Teen Island" can seem like one long party, but if you don't set up your shelter, sooner or later it's going to rain. In other words, take the time out to organise your study routine. It will not only give you a strong foundation on which to build your future, you will also find that if you do it right the first time, you will save stress later on.

Survival Equipment:
These life-rafts will keep you afloat in your busy life.
Complete the checklist to see how organised you are.

ITEM	CHECK
A large-sized calendar for your desk or wall. (One that shows a school term per page is handy.)	☐
A good alarm clock by your bedside.	☐
A diary (a week per page is good).	☐
A "Things To Do" notepad.	☐
A well-lit, quiet desk for homework.	☐
A good supply of stationery at school and at home, **with spares of pencils, pens and rulers.**	☐

> Move with the tides
> - create a routine,
> but prepare for
> the odd storm.

> The right shelter
> will keep you out
> of the swelter.

Time Management:

☐ Mark your calendar using highlighters and different coloured pens. Include assignment due dates, exam weeks, study breaks, holidays and other major events. Mark off when you will begin studying for what, so that you can plan ahead.

☐ Take your diary everywhere with you and always fill it out as you go.

☐ Use a "Things To Do" note pad each night to set out your study goals in more detail.

☐ Set your alarm clock so that you get into a regular sleep pattern, and wake up early enough to be organised in the mornings. Everyone needs different amounts of sleep to function well. Work out what you need and stick to it.

☐ Before you go to bed each night, check that you have done all your homework and put everything for the next day into your bag.

☐ Prepare for the unexpected. Never leave your homework until the last minute. If an assignment is due on Friday, aim to get it done by Wednesday. That way, if you fall ill on Thursday you will not have to beg for an extension.

Be Prepared

Setting the Environment:

☐ Pick a place to study that is light, well-aired, spacious and comfortable. Find a place in your home where all you do is study (not the same place where you watch TV or entertain friends). It will be easier to get into "work mode" when you are in that place.

☐ Make sure you have everything you need at the start of each study session. Having a separate stationery set at home might be useful.

☐ Try aromatherapy. Oils which are thought to aid memory and concentration include basil, lemon, peppermint and rosemary. Take care with oil burners and never leave them unattended. If you prefer sounds to scents, raid your parents' CD collection for some relaxing music. Many say that this helps you to study when played in the background. Classical is best. Hip-hop does not have the same effect!

DO NOT USE AEROSOLS

IN A CONFINED SPACE
It can be dangerous, always ensure the space is ventilated. If the space is not ventilated, a heat source can cause an explosion.

Handling Homework

Imagine if you let your survival camp slowly disintegrate. It might be fine while the sun is shining, but when the storms arrive, you may be swept away. Keep your brain in good condition with homework and you will be prepared for the tidal wave of exams.

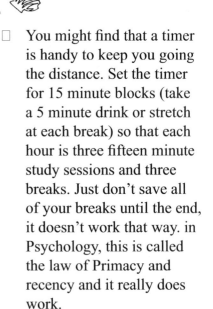

- ☐ Begin your study routine from the start of the year. If you get used to a regular pattern, it will be a lot less traumatic later on.

- ☐ Set realistic goals for yourself and treat yourself when you have reached each goal, for example, a mini chocolate bar each time you complete all your set homework.

- ☐ Take regular breaks when studying. A good one is to go and get a glass of water (it is important to keep your fluids up), or having a quick stretch will help you to sit more comfortably.

- ☐ Write your homework goals in order or priority then cover them up, only revealing one at a time, and crossing them off as soon as you have done them.

- ☐ Overestimate how much time you think it will take to complete each piece of work. Things often take longer than you expect. If you take less time than you plan for, then you will feel good about your progress, instead of disappointed.

- ☐ You might find that a timer is handy to keep you going the distance. Set the timer for 15 minute blocks (take a 5 minute drink or stretch at each break) so that each hour is three fifteen minute study sessions and three breaks. Just don't save all of your breaks until the end, it doesn't work that way. in Psychology, this is called the law of Primacy and recency and it really does work.

- ☐ Do not be disappointed in yourself if you have a bad study day. This happens to everyone. Get back into your regular routine the next day and reward yourself.

- ☐ Un-clutter your homework with a separate drawing pad if you like to sketch or scribble.

Looking After Yourself:

Survival Mission 5

When you find a good coconut on the island, eat it.

☐ Do at least one form of sport or exercise on a regular basis. Exercise is a great way to keep your mood and concentration in good form, as well as keeping you

☐ Eat well-balanced meals and use meal-time as a study break. If you need to snack when studying, choose small portions of healthy snacks such as fruit or nuts, as these will give you a natural energy boost.

☐ Try yoga or another form of relaxation, or just learn simple breathing/relaxation strategies, such as breathing in for 4 counts and out for 4, through your nose. Repeat 10 times with eyes closed, focusing on the breath filling your whole chest, down to your tummy.

☐ It's OK to have fun. As long as you have made a real effort with your work, allow yourself the reward of going to your best friend's birthday or your school ball. If you deny yourself any fun, you will probably find it difficult to study anyway.

For more ideas visit ☐www.studygs.net and read☐Study skills by John Kennedy from Studymates

SURVIVAL: TEEN ISLAND
The ultimate survival guide for 15 - 18 year olds.

15

Taking & Making Notes at School.

Imagine that Robinson Crusoe or a reality-show island survivor visited you for an hour to give you some tips. How are you going to remember all the information? Students hear an enormous amount of facts and concepts in any given day. Take note of these strategies and you will be able to pinpoint the "must know" information.

Survival Equipment:
Each student will have their own system that suits them the best.
Below are some ideas.

ITEM	CHECK
Loose, reinforced paper or a pad of hole-punched paper.	☐
A file for each subject, with notes in sequential order (dated).	☐
Coloured pens and highlighters.	☐
Something to keep notes in each day, such as a clipboard or a small file.	☐
'Post-it' pads for marking notes or book chapters.	☐

Note-taking Strategies:

Outwit your competition.

Make a habit of dating each page of notes and writing the subject at the top of the page. This will help you sort the notes out at the end of each day and keep them in order for study.

Write legibly. It is better to have less notes written neatly than a page of scrawl that you can't decipher later on.

Use a different coloured pen for headings and have a highlighter handy to emphasise important information straight away.

Use abbreviations, but keep them consistent. Write the full term the first time, with the abbreviation in brackets, e.g. "Digestive System" (dig. sys.). You can then use "dig. sys." for the rest of your notes.

Don't try and write down everything – you will miss the overall point if you get caught up in minor details. Just listen for the main points – things that your teacher repeats, says with a more expressive tone or writes up on the board.

Skim-read chapters before the lesson. This will give you some background knowledge and help you to "tune in".

Read your notes the night you take them. This will help you to absorb the facts. Not much will be retained if you just write notes during class and then open them again at exam time. For extra reinforcement, add notes/summaries from your textbooks to the notes you took in class.

Keep your notes organised. You may have a file or note book for each subject – make sure to put your notes into the correct file every night. This will only take a few minutes and will prevent the trauma of having to organise a huge amount of notes later on.

If you are finding it really hard to take notes, ask your teacher to keep a small tape recorder on his/her desk, and collect the tape after class. This way you can take notes at home but your classmates do not need to know anything about it.

Memory Strategies

Your brain is like a tropical island – it might seem inhabited but there are many unexplored areas. Use these strategies to uncover buried memories, and you will reap the rewards of many treasures.

Mnemonics:

Use these to recall lists, headings and the order of things. E.g. for the body systems: "Nervous, Lymphatic, Musculoskeletal, Digestive, Endocrine, Reproductive, Cardiovascular" use: "Never let my dog encounter rough cats".

Recite and Write:

Read a section of your own study notes, cover it up, say the information out aloud, write down what you can remember, uncover and check. If you missed a lot of information, repeat the exercise.

Study Groups:

Form a group with other students that you work well with. Some study groups work well by allocating a unit/chapter for each person to summarise. Other groups get together to test each other or discuss major learning points.

Teach Others:

Pretend your mum, dad or sibling is a student in your class who has been away all term and teach them the unit you are studying. Explaining something to another person is one of the best ways to learn and understand information.

Draw:

Many people are visual learners and remember information that is presented in tables, charts or pictures. Use colour coding and symbols in simple diagrams. Draw a scene from history.

Use a diagram to show how a formula works. Draw Mind maps, google mind maps for free software.

Rhyme, rap or sing:

Use your musical talents to make music out of the main points. Words in a song usually flow quite easily and can be used as a memory jogger.

Summarise:

When you are learning a lot of information, it helps to summarise the main ideas and use key words as headings. These key words are often enough to unlock the rest of the information that you have learned.

Make up questions:

Read through your study notes and imagine that you are the examiner. Write your own questions, cover your notes and write an answer, then mark your own work. One of the biggest secrets to successful studying is having a good idea of what will be asked during a test.

A brainstorm:

Basically, a brainstorm is a list of the most important words and concepts that you need to know from a particular topic, with lines showing how they are linked. This can be checked for a last-minute refresher just before you enter a test or exam. It might even help to draw the brainstorm as soon as you begin the test, and then refer to it later on when you get a question on that subject.

Location learning:

Stick lists and formulas on the toilet door, the fridge, your bedside table, the TV remote. Seeing these things frequently will give your memory a boost.

Quiz-it:

Get your helpful family members to read over your study notes and test you on the information. This will help you to really determine what you do and don't know and get you used to a test situation.

Source: ☐http://www.uic.edu/depts/ace/strategies.shtml

Exams

■ Exams are often one of the biggest survival challenges in high school. However, If you are well organised and study sensibly, you will be able to stay in High School Bay.

The weeks before:

☐ Write your exam schedule up on a wall and devise a study plan. Work out which areas will need the most study and allocate those subjects more time.

☐ Aim to have all your study notes written the week before exams so that the final week can be spent reading, revising and quizzing.

☐ Ask your teacher for help. They may not be able to give you the answers, but asking them a question like: "What are the most important things I need to study before this test?" might give you a good idea. Most teachers are reasonable and want you to succeed, so will probably help you decide what to study if you show an effort.

☐ Check your study notes with a small group of friends, and fill in any gaps. This is especially important if you have been absent from school at all.

☐ Many subjects have revision books, which can be purchased from educational bookstores (see www.studymates.co.uk). These will summarise notes and highlight relevant points. They might examine topics from a different angle to your teacher and help to fill in some gaps.

☐ Make good use of past test papers (ask your teacher if they have any of these). Many teachers use similar, if not identical questions each year. If you are studying for "the big exams", ask your teacher how you can order past exam papers.

The days before:

☐ Make sure you get plenty of rest, exercise and healthy food into you in the final week. This will keep your stress levels down and energy levels up.

☐ Talk to your family about how they can help you, by testing you, helping you with chores and making sure they don't interrupt your studying.

☐ Once you have written all your study notes, try out a variety of memory strategies and use the ones that suit you the best.

The night before:

☐ Do not fill yourself with coffee. This will only keep you up all night, unable to sleep and with a full bladder.

☐ A good night's sleep is as important as (if not more than) an extra hour of cramming. Try to stick to your ordinary routine as this will help you to sleep.

INVEST IN YOUR OWN BOOKS FOR REVISION, IT IS YOUR FUTURE.

www.aber-publishing.co.uk and

www.studymates.co.uk

Remember:

- Exams can sometimes be hyped up too much. Think about what percentage of your total mark the exam is worth – study more for the exams worth 80% than the ones worth 20% (unless you need a high mark in the 20% exam to pass overall).

- Once the exam is over, there is no point wasting your time worrying about how well you did. Put it behind you and focus on studying for the next subject.

- Most people do better in exams than what they think when they finish.

- If you found the exam extremely difficult (and you studied hard), chances are that everyone else found it hard too. Some teachers scale marks up if the overall results are low.

If all else fails, ask yourself this: "If I don't do well, will the world explode?" The answer, of course, is "No" (unless you are taking an exam in bomb diffusing). Put things into perspective and don't be too hard on yourself.

Exam Day:

☐ Arrive early, find a quiet patch of grass and relax.

☐ Bring plenty of supplies such as spare pens and pencils, ruler, etc.

☐ Make sure your equipment, such as your calculator, is working well.

☐ Don't talk about the test beforehand – others will have their own ideas and may put you off or make you nervous.

☐ Go to the toilet and have a drink before you enter. You may be allowed a bottle of water on your desk.

☐ Sit where you will be least distracted. You might find it hard to sit near the class clown who swings on the chair, the resident genius who finishes half an hour early, or your best buddy, who makes silly faces at you.

☐ Deal with anything like a wobbly desk straight away, otherwise it will bother you though the whole exam.

☐ Read and check the questions. Take note of how many you have to answer.

☐ Do the easy questions first – this will calm your nerves and give you more time to tackle the hard ones later.

☐ Check the time regularly during the exam, for example after each page of writing if you are doing an essay.

☐ Check your answers before you leave. Make sure all questions are clearly numbered and your name is on all pieces of work. Tidy up any obvious spelling errors or punctuation if you have time. This may score you one or two extra points.

☐ If you are doing an essay style exam and you are running out of time, jot down an outline of the main points you intended to cover in the remainder of your essay, so you at least show that you knew the information. This might get you some extra points.

☐ www.studygs.net/tsttak1.htm contains tips for different types of tests. If you can find out what type of questions will be in the exam, this has some good strategies.

Asking For Help

Survival Mission

Survival Strategies:

Over Here!

Teachers are like supply ships that pass by your island. If you make an effort to flag them down, they are more likely to stop and give you the help that you need. If you are struggling with your study, five minutes seeking help from a teacher could save hours of stressful study.

❑ Approach your teacher after class or during a break and ask when would be a good time to see them for some help.

❑ You might like to see your teacher with a classmate, so you can review the information that is given to you.

❑ Do not ask for help the day before a major exam – try a week before so that you have plenty of time to use the help you receive.

❑ Take along the study notes that you have developed already. Your teacher will be able to tell you if you are on the right track.

❑ Have specific questions about major points that you do not understand. A teacher will respond better to "Can you go though some examples of quadratic equations?" than to "Ummmm ... can you help me with my maths?"

❑ Ask if there are any books or resources that might help you, or if your teacher has any sample test papers that you can try.

❑ Ask your teacher if there are main areas which you should study in more detail. They may be kind enough to give you a big hint about what will be tested.

❑ Ask for any information that you may have missed out on if you were away from school.

❑ Thank your teacher for their time and help – a little respect and gratitude can go a long way.

Where to From Here?

Survival Mission 5

One day, it will be time to leave your island – and when that time comes, you might have two, three, maybe even four different boats waiting to whisk you away into the sunset, towards the big world of adulthood. But which boat do you take? HMS FE College? The Uni Cruiser? The Apprentice Ship? These decisions can be scary if you don't know where these vessels are really headed, or even what you have to do on board before you arrive at your destination.

Many students may have heard of an apprenticeship, but are not aware of the range of options and industries available. They may know the names of a few universities, but have never set foot in one. Planning a career is a complex process, but it's important to remember that even though you should think carefully about the decisions you make, you don't have to feel that you are sealing your fate forever. The opportunities for a varied career and for mature-age study mean that the choices you make are merely stepping stones, not one-way paths.

If you are having trouble thinking about your future career, some of these tips might be helpful:

Take some time to make some notes under these headings:

- ☐ Subjects at school I am good at and/or enjoy.
- ☐ Hobbies and interests outside of school.
- ☐ What is my personality? What do I value in life?
- ☐ What are my skills (physical, intellectual and interpersonal)?
- ☐ What is my desired lifestyle in five/ten/twenty year's time?

- ☐ Some general words/industries for the type of job I would like to do, e.g. helping, selling, teaching, making, creating, entertaining, solving, planning, etc.
- ☐ Specific jobs I think I would be good at or enjoy.
- ☐ Conditions I would like to work in, e.g. location, types of shifts, amount of travel, etc.
- ☐ A list or description of my dream jobs, with no limitations.

SURVIVAL: TEEN ISLAND
The ultimate survival guide for 15 - 18 year olds.

23

Choosing a Career

■ Keep these notes in an exercise book and change or add to them on Page 26 as you carry out some of the other investigations below:

❑ Be honest with yourself: Don't just go by other's opinions on what they think you can or should do. Don't underestimate your skills and talents. Don't try and force yourself to consider a career just because the rest of your family are doing it or it is a prestigious/honourable/high-income profession.
The most important aspects of a job are your ability to feel successful in that field and your ability to gain a sense of enjoyment or value from it in the long term. Remember that many people are happier earning less and living more.

❑ Careers counselling: Talk to your careers advisor at school (most schools will have one) about your options based on the information in these headings. Consider that school results often, but not always, reflect how you may perform in tertiary studies.

❑ If you are unsure about your career path, talk to your teachers and careers advisor about subjects that will give you the most options, whilst also being within your academic abilities.

❑ A professional careers counsellor (look through your local telephone directory) may also be able to offer some more specific advice, however they can be quite costly. Ring a few and ask about their background and whether they specialise in school-leavers.

❑ Read more about the types of jobs you are interested in. You might find that some jobs are not as interesting as they first appear, whilst discovering more about others that you had never thought about before. Check out these sites:

❑ http://www.prospects.ac.uk has information on the different avenues towards a future career, covering work, employment and training options. It includes information on careers advice, jobs and work, post-graduate study, salaary and conditions for certain jobs,the entry requirements, training, craeer development and there are some excellent case studies . ❑Careers online (http://www2.spaldingtoday.co.uk/sites/careers/default.htm) offers a similar service in a different style.

❑http://www.focus-info.org/ provides a profile of hundreds of occupations in the U.K. This will give a detailed description of the occupation and details of training required in each state.

❑ Through your school or parents, organise some work experience in the areas you are interested in. If hands-on experience is not possible, perhaps you could "shadow" someone for a day or a week and observe what they do.

❑ Getting a part-time job or doing some volunteer work in the areas you are interested in will also give you some great opportunities, and you will gain financial or personal satisfaction along the way.

❑ Witch Doctor
❑ Tribe leader
❑ Hunter
❑ Other

☐ Consider the costs involved in courses that you are interested in, e.g. up-front costs, books that need to be bought, other needs such as computers and stationery, etc.

☐ Investigate how you will be financially supported in the next few years, e.g. parental support, part-time work, available scholarships, apprenticeship plans, etc. You might feel better about a decision that you are making if you know that you can manage financially.

☐ If you are interested in a certain course of study, find out where you need to attend and visit the college. You may even be lucky enough to be able to speak with some of the lecturers or students. Keep any written information together in a folder. Many of these places have open days or expos so keep your eyes and ears open, as these are a great opportunity to get lots of information in a convenient way.

☐ Investigate your options if you have an indigenous or immigrant/international background, or if you have any disabilities or learning difficulties

☐ Talk to older siblings or other relatives or friends about what life is like in an apprenticeship/college/university. They will give you a sense of what day-to-day experiences may be like.

☐ If you are undertaking an apprenticeship or further study in a new location, such as a different county, city or town, you need to think about finding accommodation and consider how the move will impact on your life.

☐ There are many employment agencies, which can help to set up apprenticeships or find the right job for you. Look in your local telephone directory for details.

☐ Try posting your details on a job-search website such as the sites listed below . You can receive regular e-mails about potential jobs – this is a good way of seeing "what's out there" in your areas of interest.

Seek Learning http://www.seeklearning.co.uk/ great

for info on careers in ICT.

Growing Ambitions ::: The Careers Speakers Matchmaking Service for Education where the workplace shares its experiences with young people. www.growingambitions.org

Career education - they say that they are 'Enthusing young people about the world of work, helping them to make the grade' - www.ltscotland.org.uk/enterpriseineducation ...

Career Change. they say 'We find many young people of school and university age, ... While the education system may have given you the qualifications you need' .. .www.careeranalysts.co.

E.ON UK - Work with young people

The new scheme is designed to encourage young people to engage with, ... of students following these career paths through university and further education, ...www.eon-uk.com

need2know - advice on student life, relationships, travel and more!Thinking of going into further education? You might be entitled to some financial help. ... Are you excited about the Olympics in the UK in 2012? .www.need2know.co.uk

Career Notes

Section Two: Community Castaway

Learning how to look for and keep a job is like being given the X on the treasure map, making it much easier to find your fortune.

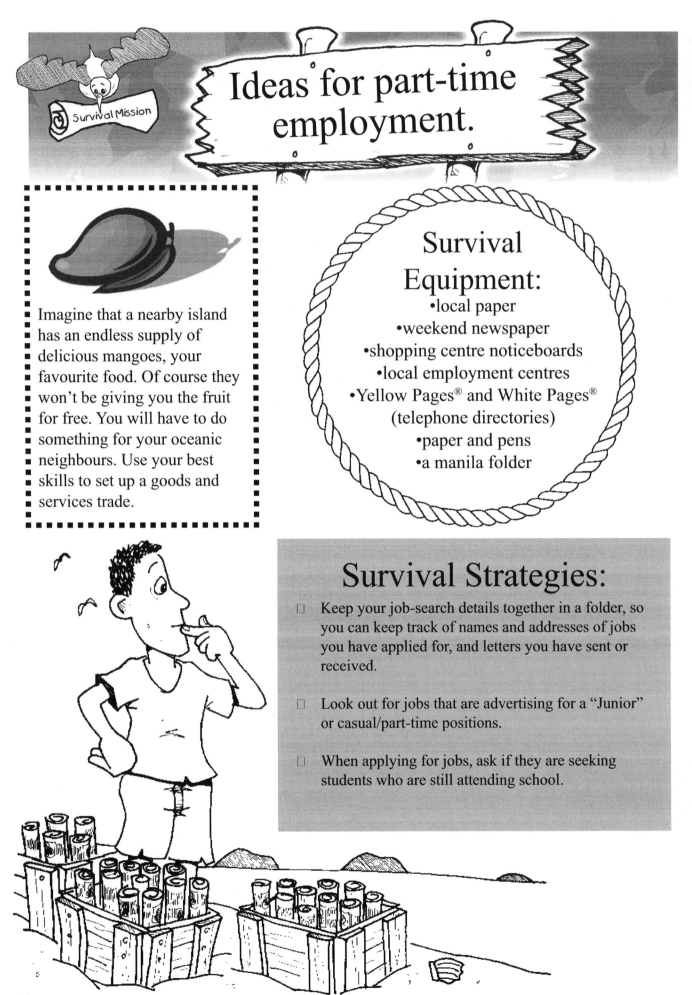

Survival Mission

Ideas for part-time employment.

Imagine that a nearby island has an endless supply of delicious mangoes, your favourite food. Of course they won't be giving you the fruit for free. You will have to do something for your oceanic neighbours. Use your best skills to set up a goods and services trade.

Survival Equipment:
- local paper
- weekend newspaper
- shopping centre noticeboards
- local employment centres
- Yellow Pages® and White Pages® (telephone directories)
- paper and pens
- a manila folder

Survival Strategies:

☐ Keep your job-search details together in a folder, so you can keep track of names and addresses of jobs you have applied for, and letters you have sent or received.

☐ Look out for jobs that are advertising for a "Junior" or casual/part-time positions.

☐ When applying for jobs, ask if they are seeking students who are still attending school.

Use your survival equipment to look out for jobs in:

• Fast food restaurants
(counter service or food preparation)
• Letter-box delivery (pamphlets or newspaper)
• Supermarkets (checkout operation or store work)
• Retail outlets
(such as clothing stores, hardware stores, etc.)
• Office junior (filing, typing, etc)
• Delicatessens
• Plant nurseries
• Odd jobs for neighbours, family, friends
(gardening, ironing, cleaning, car washing)
• Pet-walking and animal care
• Art and craft work (selling at local markets, etc.)
• Tutoring younger high school students
• Volunteer work

☐ The suggestions here are a sample of the more common options. Really, there are many more possibilities that may exist out there. Use your imagination and initiative. There is no harm in asking if part-time opportunities exist. You may even find a job that is related to the career you are interested in.

To find the job that suits you the best, think about these factors:

What are your skills, interests and hobbies?

Where is the job located?

How you will get to and from work?

What hours are you willing to work?

How much money do you want to earn?

How much time and effort are you able to put into training?

Will you need time off around exams, etc?

Will the job interfere with sport or other out-of-school commitments?

Applying For a Job

■If you want to set up a trade agreement with a neighbouring island, you must convince them that you have the best skills to give in return. Stand out from the archipelago with these tips:

There are several different ways that you can apply for a part-time job:

Cold Canvassing: This means that you are expressing interest in working somewhere even though there is not an advertised/vacant position. You can do this in three ways:

Telephone local organisations and ask about employment opportunities. This may be a good starting point if you have a range of ideas and want to narrow down the field before sending off a pile of applications. If you are going to do this, have some points about yourself written down, such as your age, what you are interested in, etc.

Ask how you should apply for any opportunities that may arise. You may be asked to send in a letter or your resume, or you may be told that there are no vacancies coming up in the near future.

Send a letter. The letter should be clear and concise, giving details about yourself and the type of employment you are looking for. This may be best following a phone call so you know who to address the letter to, and what information may be required. Include a copy of your resume/C.V. and contact details.

Visit local organisations.

This might be the best way to go if you are looking for any type of employment in a concentrated area, such as a food hall or shopping centre. Take several copies of your resume/CV with you. Some places may ask for a copy, others may simply take down a few contact details.

Responding to an advertised position:

If you see an advertisement, it will either include details on what to send and who to send it to, or it will provide a telephone contact, who will give you more information about how to apply for the job and will help you to determine if you would be a suitable candidate. Generally, an application will require you to include:

☐ A cover letter, which summarises your personal details, skills and experiences.

☐ A copy of your resume or CV. You may have done one at school or can seek help from your school careers counsellor on this. An example of the content you could include in your resume is in the next section.

☐ Contact details and details on referees. Referees could include previous employers, leaders of community clubs, family friends and teachers. You should always ask someone if they are willing to be a referee before you write them down.

☐ Many full-time and professional job advertisements also include *selection criteria*, which is a list of expected skills and experiences required for the position. Applicants are asked to write a response to each criterion, describing how their abilities and background meet the requirements.

Pick me! Pick me!

Cover Letter and C.V.

Cover Letter:

Your cover letter is like sending a message in a bottle from your island. The more clear and concise the letter is, the more likely it is that someone will come to find you!

A cover letter should be brief and should summarise your current situation and skills.

1 Find out the name of the person that you should address the letter to. Use their full name (use Mr or Mrs) and role. Also date your letter.

2 Produce your letter by clearly stating which job you wish to apply for, and where you saw it advertised.

3 Include reasons for why you want the job, but make sure they are appealing reasons such as "I am interested in gaining experience in the workforce and contributing financially to my daily living expenses" rather than "I need the money". Also give some specifics, e.g. "I have always enjoyed gardening and I am interested in a future career in horticulture".

4 Include examples of your skills/experience/interest in the area.

5 Sell yourself – outline your strengths. Below are some of the attributes that employers seek. Include some of these words in your letter: Good communication skills; Honest and reliable; A strong work ethic; Enjoy teamwork and have excellent interpersonal skills; Flexible and eager to take on additional responsibilities; Motivated to work hard and take initiative; Organised, with good time management skills.

6 End on a positive note, such as "I am happy to answer any further questions regarding my experience. Thank you for your time in considering this application".

SURVIVAL: TEEN ISLAND
The ultimate survival guide for 15 - 18 year olds

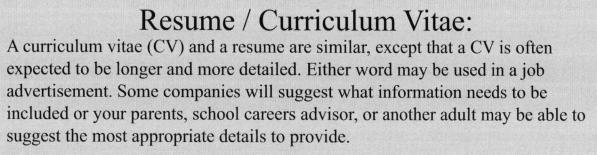

Resume / Curriculum Vitae:

A curriculum vitae (CV) and a resume are similar, except that a CV is often expected to be longer and more detailed. Either word may be used in a job advertisement. Some companies will suggest what information needs to be included or your parents, school careers advisor, or another adult may be able to suggest the most appropriate details to provide.

Here are some commonly required details:

 Your personal details: Name, address, telephone, date of birth, your gender (male or female)

 Previous employment: Details of any previous employment, such as dates worked, the job title, a brief summary of your role and responsibilities.

 Education: School attended, current year level or highest year level achieved, summary of most recent results. If you have recently completed a FE College course or training course, include this as well.

Other training: Include other experience or training which may be relevant to the job, such as First Aid certificates, etc.

Awards and positions of responsibility at school, e.g. Sports Captain, Drama Award, Student Councillor, etc.

 Sports, hobbies and interests, community participation, volunteer work, etc.

Extra Tips (for using Microsoft Word):

☐ Keep your computer and printer in good condition so that job applications are professionally presented.

☐ Choose a simple font such as Times New Roman or Arial (12 pt size).

☐ Use a simple approach for headings, such as bold print.

☐ Align or justify your text so it is centred on the page and evenly space each section.

Source: ☐http://www.winning-cvs.co.uk/cvtips.htm

Also check out http://www.e-cvs.net/tomecv/default.asp ☐

Below is an example of a cover letter from a high school student seeking a part-time job in a garden nursery. Look at the notes alongside it to see how a letter like this can be set out.

Make your contact details easy to read and quick to find.

20 Knoxville Lane
Spring Valley, LL22 8EE
Ph: 9 999 9999
E-mail: bradc@abermail.com

Date your letter.

March 17, 2009

Address the letter to the appropriate person. Use formal titles, i.e. Mr or Mrs.

Mr Robert Jones
Manager
Spring Valley Nurseries
PO Box 253
Spring Valley, LL22 8YL

Dear Mr Jones

Include the date of the advertisement and where you found it.

I am writing in response to your advertisement in The Western News on March 12 for a Junior Nursery Assistant.

Include a statement about what you are currently doing and outline why you are applying for the position.

As a Year 12 student at Spring Valley Senior High School, I am seeking part-time employment that complements my skills and interests. I am keen to pursue a career in horticulture or landscape design. Currently achieving excellent results in Biology, and cultivating my own garden at home, I am familiar with many plant varieties and gardening techniques. I have been looking for an opportunity to develop my knowledge in a dynamic environment.

I have many personal attributes, which I feel would be an asset in the nursery environment, including:

Give specific information as to why you are suited to the job. Use dot points to convey a concise summary of your key attributes and experiences.

- Leadership and Initiative: Currently Sports Captain at Spring Valley SHS.
- Excellent teamwork: Member of Spring Valley SHS Football Club and Interschool Debating Team.
- Strong Interpersonal Skills: Awarded the Citizenship Prize in Year 11.

Include statements that show you have conducted some recent research and think highly of the company with which you are applying for

On a recent visit to your nursery, I enjoyed speaking to staff about your fantastic "Outdoor Living" display. I can picture myself as a valued employee of Spring Valley Nursery who is able to quickly settle into your friendly, professional team.

Provide a rough idea of your availability without being too restrictive and thank the reader for their interest.

I am able to work afternoons from 3.30pm and weekends at any time. I have enclosed ac.v. for your information. Thank you for considering this application.

Yours sincerely

Sign off formally.

Brad Cooper

Brad Cooper

Enc. c.v..

Check out Bradley's winning curriculum vitae/resume:

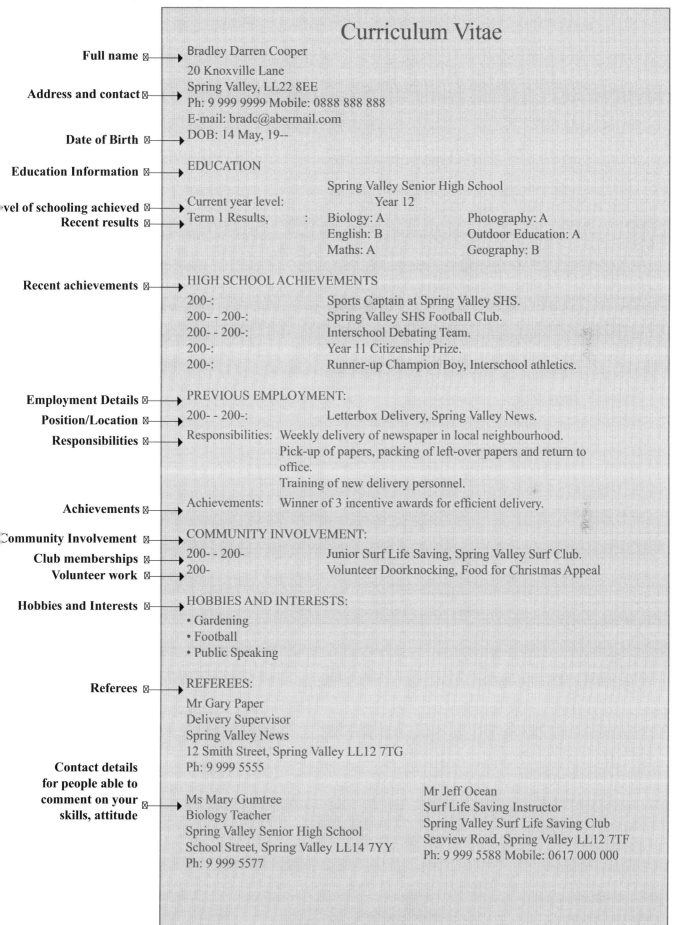

Full name ⊠ → Bradley Darren Cooper

Address and contact ⊠ → 20 Knoxville Lane
Spring Valley, LL22 8EE
Ph: 9 999 9999 Mobile: 0888 888 888
E-mail: bradc@abermail.com

Date of Birth ⊠ → DOB: 14 May, 19--

Education Information ⊠ → EDUCATION

Spring Valley Senior High School

vel of schooling achieved ⊠ → Current year level: Year 12
Recent results ⊠ → Term 1 Results,   :   Biology: A   Photography: A
English: B   Outdoor Education: A
Maths: A   Geography: B

Recent achievements ⊠ → HIGH SCHOOL ACHIEVEMENTS

200-:   Sports Captain at Spring Valley SHS.
200- - 200-:   Spring Valley SHS Football Club.
200- - 200-:   Interschool Debating Team.
200-:   Year 11 Citizenship Prize.
200-:   Runner-up Champion Boy, Interschool athletics.

Employment Details ⊠ → PREVIOUS EMPLOYMENT:

Position/Location ⊠ → 200- - 200-:   Letterbox Delivery, Spring Valley News.

Responsibilities ⊠ → Responsibilities: Weekly delivery of newspaper in local neighbourhood.
Pick-up of papers, packing of left-over papers and return to office.
Training of new delivery personnel.

Achievements ⊠ → Achievements: Winner of 3 incentive awards for efficient delivery.

Community Involvement ⊠ → COMMUNITY INVOLVEMENT:

Club memberships ⊠ → 200- - 200-   Junior Surf Life Saving, Spring Valley Surf Club.
Volunteer work ⊠ → 200-   Volunteer Doorknocking, Food for Christmas Appeal

Hobbies and Interests ⊠ → HOBBIES AND INTERESTS:

• Gardening
• Football
• Public Speaking

Referees ⊠ → REFEREES:

Mr Gary Paper
Delivery Supervisor
Spring Valley News
12 Smith Street, Spring Valley LL12 7TG
Ph: 9 999 5555

**Contact details
for people able to
comment on your
skills, attitude** ⊠ → Ms Mary Gumtree
Biology Teacher
Spring Valley Senior High School
School Street, Spring Valley LL14 7YY
Ph: 9 999 5577

Mr Jeff Ocean
Surf Life Saving Instructor
Spring Valley Surf Life Saving Club
Seaview Road, Spring Valley LL12 7TF
Ph: 9 999 5588 Mobile: 0617 000 000

Curriculum Vitae

Part-time job interview.

Survival Mission

So, you scored an interview? Well done! Now, keep in mind that you will be visiting another island and you must make a good impression with how you speak, what you bring and what you wear. Interviews can range from an informal chat with one person, to a formal panel interview, where two or three people are asking questions. Some interviews might give you the questions in advance and a short time to prepare your answers.

Survival Equipment:

Check these items off before you go. Take everything in a professional-looking bag that is easy to open and locate things.

ITEM	CHECK
A copy of your application and CV.	☒
School records and awards. Order them in a folder with the most recent and most impressive records at the front.	☒
Certificates or examples of work that relate to the job.	☒
	☒
Contact details for referees.	☒
Small pad and a pen to write information down.	
A small bottle of water for that dry throat, and a tissue in case of a sniffle.	☒
Write any other items you need to bring: _____	

Survival Strategies:

❑ Phone up in advance to find out: How to get there (where to park or get off public transport); where to report (e.g. front desk); who to ask for (who will be interviewing you?) and anything you need to bring (this will probably give you an idea of how formal the interview will be).

❑ Dress for the interview. Wear smart, neat, clean clothes, sensible shoes, neutral or simple colours, tidy hair. No excessive make-up if you are a girl, and the less flesh showing, the better! When planning your outfit, prepare for the weather – you don't want to come in looking like a drowned rat or have sweaty armpit marks!

❑ Arrive 5 - 10 minutes early to allow yourself time to find the place, sit down to relax and prepare.

❑ Have some questions prepared, but make sure they are sensible and relevant to the job.

Training Activities

Write some answers to the questions below, plus write some others that you think the interviewer may ask. Practise responding with a friend or family member.

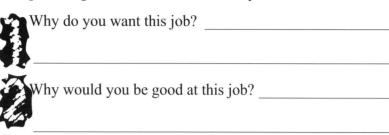 Why do you want this job? _____

_____

Why would you be good at this job? _____

_____

What are your strengths and weaknesses? _____

_____

How do you work in a team situation? _____

_____

☐ Try to give examples for your answers, e.g. If you are asked about your time management skills, you might say "I keep a diary for my homework at school and I do an hour of homework each night before I watch TV."

☐ Try on your interview outfit the night before the interview to make sure it looks OK.

☐ Try different sitting postures in front of the mirror so you can make sure you are not slouching, swinging your feet, etc.

You are sitting in front of the interview panel. Don't be afraid – the interviewers might be from another island but they are still in the same sea. In other words, they are people too, and just as anxious about finding someone as you are about getting the job. Relax and tell yourself "If I am the right person, I will get the job."

During the interview:

- Smile and make eye contact.

- Sit upright but comfortably in the chair.

- Wait until you are invited to enter a room, shake hands, sit down, etc.

- Remember the names of the interviewers. If you repeat their names at the end, e.g. "Thank you for this opportunity, Mr Jones", or "It was lovely to meet you, Sally", you will impress.

- Don't fidget or chew gum. These things are very off-putting.

- You might be asked how many hours you would like to work per week, so think about what you could handle. Be enthusiastic but realistic, and be prepared to work weekends and/or evenings if the job requires this.

- Turn off your mobile!

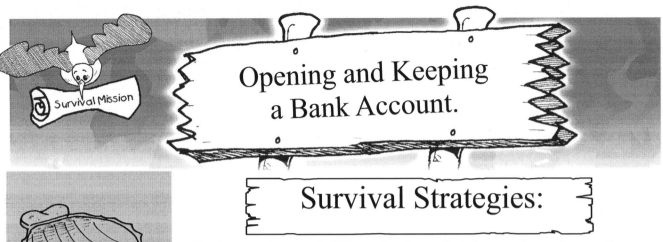

Opening and Keeping a Bank Account.

Survival Strategies:

- ☐ Approach several different banks to find the one that suits you the best.

- ☐ You may have an existing account, opened by your parents, at a bank already. Find out what the account can offer you.

- ☐ Ask the advice of family and friends: Which bank they belong to, what are the benefits and how they find the service, charges, etc.?

- ☐ Most banks will have websites which outline their services – do your homework and check these out. You will be armed with knowledge and will be able to ask the right questions.

- ☐ After looking up the location of a few banks in your area, the best way to get an idea of what they can offer you is to visit each one.

- ☐ Take a parent or another adult with you, so they can help to explain any concepts and assist you in making judgements on the information you receive.

- ☐ Tell the bank that you have a new part-time job and are interested in finding out about options for opening an account.

- ☐ Do not make any on-the-spot decisions. Take all the information away with you and make a thorough decision.

If you keep all your savings in a treasure chest, sooner or later the pirates will find it. Now that you have your part-time job, you might like to open a bank account to keep your money safe.

Survival Equipment: Telephone directory, parental advice

TYPES OF ACCOUNTS:

Account types and names will vary from bank to bank, but here is a basic summary of some common account

Current Accounts:

Allow you regular access to your money, with few or no limitations or fees for withdrawals. These will allow you to use ATM and EFTPOS facilities, and some have a cheque-book option as well.

Savings Accounts:

Can help you meet savings goals by giving good interest rates. These are good for people who want to put money into the account regularly and not take money out very often.

Cheque Accounts:

Similar to savings accounts, but also include a cheque book which can be used to pay for items and bills by cheque.

Term Deposit Accounts:

This is best for a large amount of money that is placed in an account. You can earn fixed interest over a term that you specify. This is good if you want to use the interest that you earn but do not want access to the account itself. Interest can be paid at a term that you choose, such as monthly, quarterly (every 3 months), half-yearly or annually.

Ask About:

☐ The ways that you can do your banking, e.g. telephone or Internet banking.

☐ Future options, for when you are a full-time worker.

Bring:

☐ Some identification, such as passport or birth certificate;

☐ Information on your new job such as address and contact details;

☐ Paper and pen to write things down;

☐ Plastic sleeves to keep information about each bank separate.

Saving and Budgeting

■ The best survivors are those who ration their supplies. You never know what the future holds so it is best to put some of your savings aside in case of a rainy day.

Survival Strategies:

☐ Make a Wish-list of things that you would like to buy. Put them into two columns, Things I Need and Things I Want. Next to each item use a key which prioritises how important it is that you have the item, e.g.

* = Not very important
** = Medium importance
*** = Highly Important

☐ Keep a budget for a few weeks to find out what you normally spend. Write down everything you buy with your own money.

☐ Look back over your budget. How many things on your Wish-list are you able to buy? How much money are you saving each week? How much would you like to save each week?

☐ Mark all the things on your budget which you are willing to sacrifice. Common items include junk food, expensive gifts, magazines, accessories, music, mobile telephone bills.

☐ Take these away from your weekly spending, compare to your weekly income and work out how much you should be able to save each week.

☐ Draw up a new budget, with your weekly spending and saving plan. Trial this for 3 - 4 weeks and make any adjustments.

☐ Enjoy spending your savings on items from your Wish-list.

☐ If you are wishing to save for a large purchase, consider a pound-for-pound/ Euro-for euro(or similar) plan where your parents contribute a proportional amount for every pound/Euro that is saved.

Survival Equipment:

• A good bank account

• Some willpower

SURVIVAL: TEEN ISLAND
The ultimate survival guide for 15 - 18 year olds

Check Out Jo's 'Before and After'

The calculations here are for a British student, if you are in Europe just substitute Euros for pounds and the same maths works

☐ Highlighted items are those that Jo thinks she does not really need to spend so much money on.

WEEK 1

Weekly Income: £ 60.00

Item	Cost
Expenditure	
Magazine	£2.95
Mobile phone	£4.50
Snacks	£7.00
T-shirt	£8.00
Drinks	£9.20
Movie Ticket	£5.00
Hair Clip	£2.40
Lip Gloss	£1.50
CD Single	£7.00
Lunch	£5.60
DVD hire	£6.00
Total Spent	£59.15
Total Savings	£0.85

WEEK 2

Weekly Income:£60

Item	Cost
Expenditure	
Mobile Phone	£2.00
Snacks	£1.20
Movie Ticket	£5.00
CD	£1.50
Mini Golf	£1.50
Total Spent	£11.20
Total Savings	£48.80

Wish-list	Price
Wants	
New CD***	£27.00
Shoes *	£56.00
Stereo**	£230.00
Birthday Present **	£20.00
Concert Tickets***	£46.00
Needs	
School Bag*	£15.00

*not very important
**medium important
***very important

Jo's Savings Plan

- Mainly take lunch and snacks from home instead of eating out.

- Reduce pointless text messages on mobile. Switch to cheaper plan.

- Borrow DVDs off friends instead of hiring them.

- Stop buying accessories – I have too many already.

- Use movie ticket voucher book and other vouchers for entertainment.

- Swap old magazines with friends instead of buying new ones. Take magazine buying in turns.

Jo saved £48.80 in her first week and has already managed to buy the first item on her Wish- list. If she saves this amount for the next three weeks, she can afford those concert tickets and those fantastic new shoes, with plenty of change left over.

Using a Credit Card

Most banks and credit unions offer credit cards, which are cards used to access funds that your bank has loaned to you on the condition that you will pay them back. Some major department stores even offer credit cards, however, these cards are generally attached to an external financial institution. Examples of credit cards include Master Card, Visa and American Express. Credit cards have a credit limit so that you can only draw as much money as the lending institution will allow. This sum is determined when you first sign up for a credit card and the amount is calculated based on your ability to pay off the credit amount. Other factors that influence the credit limit include the type of card you apply for and how often you are able to make repayments. Most credit cards require a monthly repayment to be paid into the account.

Credit cards are NOT free money.

They are often high interest loans in disguise.

Credit card companies make their money by charging interest on the amount borrowed. How much interest you pay depends on how long it takes you to pay what you owe.

As well as charging interest on your purchases, many cards charge an annual fee. The interest rate can be as high as 30% with some finance cards associated with department stores having rates between 30-40%. Some cards allow you to withdraw cash (a cash advance) as well as making purchases. However, cash advance fees can also add up and the interest rate for cash advances is usually higher than the interest rate for purchases on actual items. Many cards also charge a late payment fee when people miss a repayment.

Adding the Costs Up

Example

Jenny spent £100 on clothes using her credit card. The interest rate on her card was 18%. The annual fee was £40 and she missed her first repayment and was charged a late fee of £20. All up, Jenny owed £18 in interest so she was paying £118 for items that were only worth £100. Her total credit card bill had soared to £178 and she still hadn't paid for any of her purchases!

Being Credit Smart

Things to remember when signing up for a credit card:

- You, and only you, will be responsible for paying the bills.

- Read all the application materials and forms very carefully – YES, this means the fine print.

- Note that many credit cards offer a special low interest rate for new customers as an introductory offer. Some will advertise an interest rate for as low as 5% when in fact after the introductory period is over, the rate can soar to as high as 30%.

- Find out what happens to your interest rate if you're late with a payment or fail to make a payment. Also, find out the interest rate for a cash advance.

- Consider using a debit card instead of a credit card. This means that money is deducted directly from your checking or savings account, so you can't spend more than you actually have.

- Only use your card if you are sure that you are able to meet the repayments.

- Don't buy things on impulse just because you have your credit card with you.

- Save your credit card for a money emergency. Do not use your card to pay for things like a holiday or a night out with friends.

- Pay your credit card bill on time. Even if you can't pay the entire balance, at least pay the minimum monthly repayment to avoid paying a late fee.

Getting a Good Credit Rating

When the time comes for you to apply for a loan for either a car, a house or even a business loan, you will need a good credit rating. Problems with credit cards, such as missed or late repayments can go as a black mark against your name and you may have difficulty securing a loan. All banks and lending institutions will have access to your credit rating so you cannot simply go to a different bank to escape a bad credit rating.

Want to know more?
Check this site out for details on finding the right credit card for your needs:
http://www.moneysavingexpert.com/cards/credit-cards-main-guide

Section Three:
Social Smoke Signals

Fine-tune your communication skills and you'll get more out of the other islanders.

E-mails
Formal v Informal

E-MAILS – the modern-day answer to smoke signals – are the best way to get an instant message to anyone, whether they are across the road or across the world. In formal or business situations, an e-mail should be treated like a letter. E-mails are often kept on file as records and should look professional.

☐ Do

☐ Learn how to use the attachment function and include a message in the e-mail explaining the attachment.

☐ Only send to the correct person.

☐ Keep the subject line short and relevant.

☐ Use a formal introduction for adults in business.

☐ Message is brief, polite and to the point.

☐ Use punctuation correctly for a professional finish.

☐ Using a "signature" will look good and provide the reader with all your contact details right in front of them.

Junior Store-person Application

File   Edit   View   Insert   Format   Tools   Message   Help

Send   Cut   Copy   Paste   Undo   Check   Spelling   Attach   ❶

From: Joseph@teenisland.com

❷ To: djones@worklink.com

Cc:

❸ Subject: Junior Store-person Application

B I U A

❹ Dear Mr Jones

Re: Junior Store-person Application

❺ Please find attached a cover letter and resume in response to the Junior Store-person advertisement from the Smallville Times,

❻ June 18th.

Yours sincerely

Joseph Bloggs
12 Smart Street
Smallville LL18 9JJ
Ph: 0 222 6666

Edit   Source   Preview

New Message

| File | Edit | View | Insert | Format | Tools | Message | Help |

Send | Cut | Copy | Paste | Undo | Check | Spelling | Attach

From: mybestfriend@worklink.com

To: djones@worklink.com

Cc:

Subject: ☐

Arial | 10 | B I U A |

❷ hi Dave

❸ i am writing to apply for the junior store person's job.

❹ call me whenever for more info

❺ I CAN WORK THURSDAYS, SATURDAYS AND SUNDAYS.

☒ Joe :)

Edit | Source | Preview

☐ Don't

☐ If you leave the subject line blank, the e-mail could be ignored or deleted.

☐ Do not use informal introductions until the other person has let you know that this is acceptable.

☐ Lack of punctuation and use of abbreviation makes the e-mail look sloppy and the writer lazy.

☐ What is Joe's number? Should he really be expecting a call anyway?

☐ Capital letters make it seem like you are shouting.

☐ There is no reference to the attachment. It may be overlooked.

☐ Save smileys for your friends. A potential employer reading this would not be smiling!

Other Netiquette Pointers:

oh ohh...

THE NUMBER ONE RULE:

Always check your e-mail before clicking *Send*. Check who you are sending it to, (click the right button, e.g. Did you click "reply" or "reply all"?). Check the whole e-mail, including what you have quoted, copied or pasted. Make sure you have an appropriate subject line.

SURVIVAL: TEEN ISLAND
The ultimate survival guide for 15 - 18 year olds .

45

Other Netiquette Pointers:

Maintenance:

Tidy up your inbox frequently by deleting old e-mails, especially items such as jokes and images. Keep important e-mails in organised folders for easy retrieval. Learn how to use address books, distribution lists and filters. These will save you time and hassles.

Spelling:

Ewes a spell cheque system if your e male system has won, butt bare in mined that it mite knot sea awl of you're miss steaks. In other words, check for errors by reading your e-mail instead of just relying on the spell-check system. A thesaurus is available on many e-mail systems and will help you find some impressive words for any situation.

Sending:

Make sure you read over the e-mail and delete any personal or rude information – it will come back to bite you – some people save e-mails for years! Before you send an e-mail, ask yourself "Would I say this to the person face to face?" If the answer is "No", then you should consider revising what you have written.

Don't send super-long messages to friends on holidays. They may be in an e-mail café that is costing them £5 for half an hour, and they don't have time to trawl through countless messages.

Replying:

If you are having an e-mail "conversation" with someone and continue to click on "Reply", try to delete some of the earlier conversation. This will prevent your messages from taking up too much room and will cut out irrelevant information. If the person sending the e-mail asked you lots of questions perhaps quote them (by copying and pasting their question into your text) so they know what you are responding to. For example: You asked me "Are you going to the football game on Sunday?" Yes, I am going if I can get tickets at the gates.

Forwarding:

Do not forward another person's message without their permission – it would be like posting a personal letter up on a communal notice board.

It is polite to ask people permission before sending a large e-mail forward, as these can clog up valuable space and sit in an inbox for weeks before being opened. Try a simple warning: "I have some great pictures from the school ball. Do you want me to e-mail them to you?"

Chat Rooms:

Be very wary and never give out personal information like your full name, address or phone number to someone you do not know. Some "whackos" out there will pretend to be someone that they are not, and could have dangerous intentions.

Cut the Chain:

Some e-mails, such as "chain e-mails" are just plain annoying, especially those ones that say something like "Send this e-mail to five people you love and good luck will come your way". Do you really believe that? If in doubt, chuck it out!

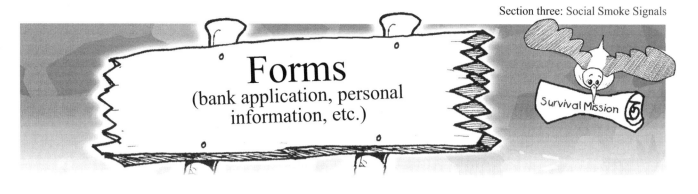

Forms
(bank application, personal information, etc.)

Survival Mission 5

■ Your chances of survival in the big wide world are increased when you fill out forms properly so that your personal details are accurate and consistent.

Use these tips for an efficient outcome when filling out any kind of form.

Keep the details below in a safe but accessible place, as you will often need these details for filling out forms:

☐ Names and addresses of emergency contacts (your neighbour, aunt, family friend, etc.).

☐ Your passport number (if you have one).

☐ Your drivers' licence number (if you have one).

☐ Bank details (The name of your bank, the branch, your bank sort code and account number, your account type).

☐ Your national insurance number.

☐ The name and address and contact details of your employer and previous employers.

☐ Names and contact details of anyone that may be able to give a personal reference.

DO NOT give your bank account details to an online request. It may be a phishing email designed to steal your money. Banks and Ebay never ask for online details.

When filling out a form:

☐ Use a blue or a black pen only. Pencil or other coloured pens are hard to photocopy.

☐ Write in block capitals, especially if you are writing one letter per box. This will make it easier to read.

☐ If you make a mistake, cross it out and sign your correction with your initials. Better still – get a new form.

☐ If you can, keep a copy of the form you have filled out for your own reference.

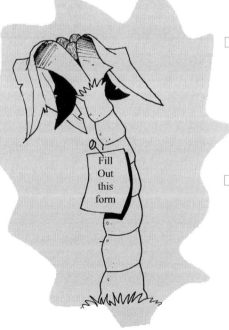

Fill Out this form

Important points to remember:

☐ If you fill out a competition form that asks for your name, age, address, school and a photo, people could use this information in an incorrect way. Some companies might use your information to give to another organisation, they may send you an annoying amount of junk mail or make a number of marketing telephone calls to your home.

☐ Always get a parent to check your form before submitting it. If you are under 18, many forms will require you to have an adult signature on it.

☐ **Warning: be extremely wary of online forms, especially ones that ask for a lot of personal or bank details. Always get an adult to assist you with these situations.**

☐ If you are filling out an online form, you may be able to print off a version first so you can take your time filling it out, check your information and run it by one of your parents before filling it out online.

SURVIVAL: TEEN ISLAND
The ultimate survival guide for 15 - 18 year olds .

47

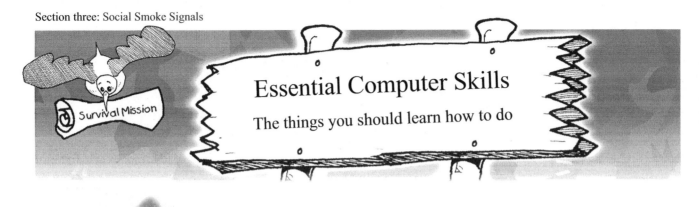

Essential Computer Skills
The things you should learn how to do

On an island, an essential skill might be building a fire, which enables you to carry out many other tasks. In the workforce, computer skills are of the same importance.

SCORE 1 POINT FOR EACH ITEM YOU TICK:

☒ I know how to turn a computer on. (If you don't know this, you probably shouldn't read the rest of the page!)

☒ I know the difference between hardware and software.

☒ I can use a standard program such as MS Word® to produce a written document.

☒ I can use a program such as Power Point® to create a presentation for a project.

☒ I am able to use at least one or more of the other software applications below: Software for processing and presenting data (e.g. graphs, etc.); Packages for drawing or presenting graphics for birthday cards, banners, etc.; Software for learning new information (e.g. encyclopaedia CDs); game software; virus protection software.

☒ I can send an e-mail with attachments to another person.

☒ I keep folders of all my e-mail messages, maintaining a tidy inbox, with weekly or monthly cleanouts; and maintain an e-mail address book with different distribution lists, e.g. "school friends".

☒ I know what to do if the computer freezes.

☒ I can use and maintain a printer, including re-inking and cleaning

☒ I can use a scanner and digital camera.

☒ I can search the Internet by using a search engine and navigating web pages, e.g. being able to return to home pages, use correct key words and phrases to refine and direct my search, e.g. using quotation marks for exact phrases.

☒ I bookmark my favourite sites.

☒ I maintain and back up my hard drive and desktop documents.

☒ I know different ways to save my documents, e.g. to a folder, onto the desktop, onto a disk (floppy or CD), onto a network; and I understand how some of these can interrelate.

☒ I know the difference between a readable only CD and a readable/writeable one.

NOW ADD UP YOUR

0-1	**Much more to learn**
2-5	**Getting there**
6-10	**Computer savvy**
11-15	**Tech Wiz**

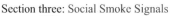

Telephone Skills
for speaking to adults in formal & informal situations

Survival Mission 5

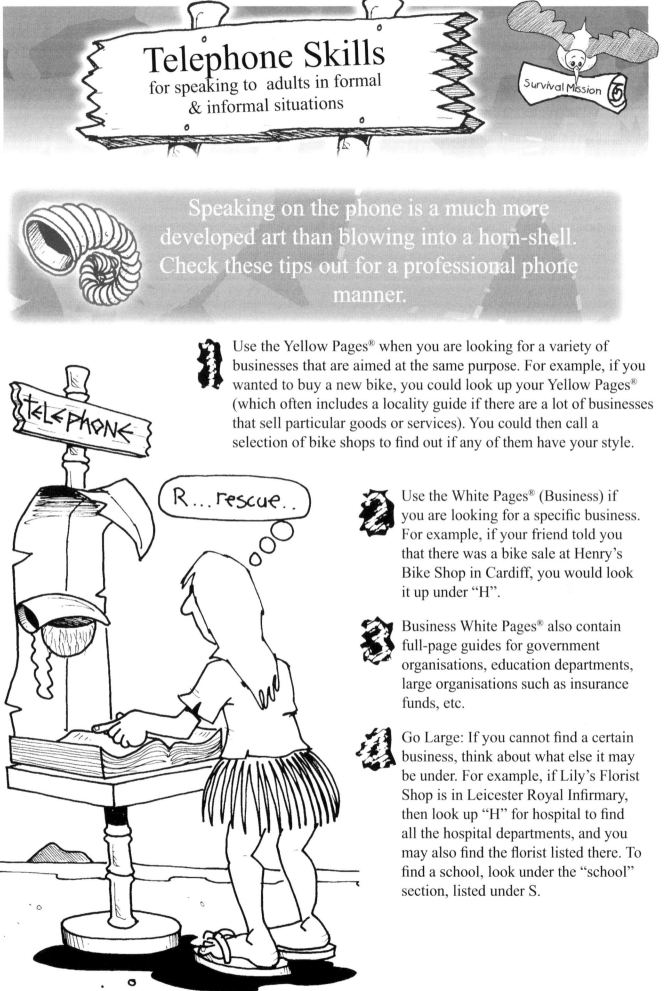

Speaking on the phone is a much more developed art than blowing into a horn-shell. Check these tips out for a professional phone manner.

1. Use the Yellow Pages® when you are looking for a variety of businesses that are aimed at the same purpose. For example, if you wanted to buy a new bike, you could look up your Yellow Pages® (which often includes a locality guide if there are a lot of businesses that sell particular goods or services). You could then call a selection of bike shops to find out if any of them have your style.

2. Use the White Pages® (Business) if you are looking for a specific business. For example, if your friend told you that there was a bike sale at Henry's Bike Shop in Cardiff, you would look it up under "H".

3. Business White Pages® also contain full-page guides for government organisations, education departments, large organisations such as insurance funds, etc.

4. Go Large: If you cannot find a certain business, think about what else it may be under. For example, if Lily's Florist Shop is in Leicester Royal Infirmary, then look up "H" for hospital to find all the hospital departments, and you may also find the florist listed there. To find a school, look under the "school" section, listed under S.

SURVIVAL: TEEN ISLAND
The ultimate survival guide for 15 - 18 year olds .

49

Making Calls

Professional Calls:

If you are phoning to find out specific information, arm yourself with a pen and paper. Write the number and name of the person who you speak to. Write any questions with a space underneath so you can easily write the answers. Go to a quiet area away from loud radios, screaming siblings and barking dogs.

Always give your name first. State your reason for calling, or the information that you are seeking, and ask whom you should speak to.

If you are put through to another person, re-introduce yourself and your purpose. You don't know how much or how little information they have been given.

It is often polite to ask; "Is this a good time to call?" especially if you are calling a mobile number.

If the person is unavailable, ask whether it would be best for them to phone you back, or for you to phone at another time. Always leave your full name, telephone number and mobile number. It may also be helpful to give some good times to call, but try and be flexible.

If you are invited to do so, leave a message which gets your point across without too much irrelevant information, for example, "I would like some more information about the part-time paper delivery job", instead of saying "I am fifteen years old and I am fit, and I have a bike – do you think I should apply for the delivery job?"

Thank the message-taker for their help, using their name. You will leave a good impression, and you never know, it could be th company director walking past someone's phone and picking it up.

Social calls:

It is still common courtesy to use parents' surnames when calling your friends, until they ask you to call them otherwise. Always say who you are and your friend's parents will like you much better.

Just make a simple comparison to "Is Scotty there?" to "Hi Mrs Scott, this is James. Can speak to Brett please?"

Answering Calls:

 It is best to answer your phone with a friendly "Hello" or "Jack speaking", rather than an aggressive "Yeah?" or a silly "Fred's Funny Farm". You never know when you will be getting an important call. A prospective employer may not have much of a sense of humour.

If you have an answering machine, make sure it is clear and includes your name, especially if you are looking for part-time work. "You have reached the Smith residence. Bill, Mary and Joseph are not available to take your call right now ..."

On The Phone:

If it is an important call and your other line rings, you may wish to ignore it. You can always use a function that searches for the last unanswered call. The second caller will phone later. Similarly, do not answer your mobile whilst on an important landline call.

Don't eat, drink or do other distracting tasks such as washing the dishes when making important phone calls.

According to many sources, if you smile when you are speaking on the phone, people can hear it. It certainly wouldn't hurt to try.

SURVIVAL: TEEN ISLAND
The ultimate survival guide for 15 - 18 year olds .

51

Survival Mission

Driving Cars

Earning your drivers' licence is like getting a great little boat to explore the other islands around you, and even venture further out into the big, wide world.

Here are a few driver reminders to keep you and other drivers safe.

☐ Not wearing a seatbelt is a fineable offence.

☐ If you break driving laws too many times, you will have your licence withdarwn.

☐ You will cop a fine when you commit a driving offence, so you lose pounds as well as collect points on your licence.

☐ If you are caught driving under the influence of alcohol, you will be fined, lose your licence and it will be recorded as a criminal offence.

☐ If you injure someone by having an accident while driving under the influence, you could face serious criminal charges, not to mention the guilt that will probably haunt you for the rest of your life.

☐ Apart from alcohol, other high contributors to driving deaths are speed, fatigue and not wearing seatbelts.

☐ Road rage is becoming more of a problem in today's hectic society. Don't contribute to the problem by honking, gesturing or pulling faces. You really don't know how aggressive the other drivers can get. If you are feeling uncomfortable, lock your door and wind your window up. If you are simply feeling annoyed at reckless driving, pull back and imagine that there just might be a cop around the corner, about to pull over the offender.

☐ Speeding affects your reaction time, your stopping distance and the force at which you hit another car, a pedestrian or an object. All of these mean that the likelihood of an accident is increased, as well as the severity of that accident.

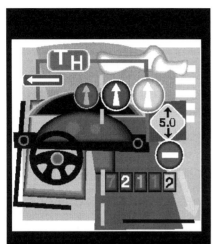

Learning how to drive is one thing, doing it well for the rest of your life is another. Young drivers are a traffic cop's field day so remember your road rules and drive in a way that protects your life and your precious wheels.

REMEMBER
A traffic cop who spots you will look for a reason to pull you over. Driving well means s/he will not have that reason.

❑ Many learners are not exposed to situations like heavy weather, peak-hour traffic, new road works, emergency vehicles, cattle or horses or domestic animals, loads falling off a trailer, late night or country driving, road trains, etc. All of these are encountered on the road and the young driver needs to know what to do.

❑ It is an offence to use a hand-held mobile phone whilst driving. This includes sending text messages. **It is incredibly dangerous and in Britain a number of people have died because of car drivers using mobile phones.**

❑ The statistics on deaths and severe injuries in young drivers are quite distressing.

❑ Practise being confident in telling your friends when you don't feel comfortable having passengers if you think they will cause a distraction. Make a pact with them that if the driver calls for silence, it is to be given immediately. Drinking, shouting, moving around, putting limbs out of the car, passengers touching controls (even the radio or air conditioner) can all cause major distractions. If your passengers are doing any of these things, stop the car and refuse to start again until the passengers have promised to behave. A bit of ribbing from your mates is worth your lives.

❑ Make sure you buy a car that is mechanically sound. As a guarantee, have your car checked out by the RAC or AA and get it regularly serviced. Also learn how to do the basics yourself, like topping up oil and water and putting air into the tyres. Even the best driver can be affected more seriously if their car is not up to scratch.

Sources

❑ www.lsite.vicroads.vic.gov.au/index2.html
❑ www.officeofroadsafety.wa.gov.au
❑ www.atsb.gov.au/road/newdrivers

SURVIVAL: TEEN ISLAND
The ultimate survival guide for 15 - 18 year olds .

53

Using Maps

These skills will save you a lot of time and stress, especially when you get the holy grail – your drivers' licence.

Familiarise yourself with the symbols and keys. Once you are able to identify things such as roundabouts, traffic lights, bridges, telephone boxes, parking lots, etc. you will be able to recognise landmarks and find your way around a lot quicker.

Start Here Make sure you have the map up the right way. Some people find it easier to turn the map in the direction that you are going. If you are reading upside down, then what appears on the left of your map will actually be to your right.
It sounds simple but this is a common error, even by adults who have been driving for years.

Understand how the maps in a map book join. Many maps have an overlap section so it is easier to see where you have come from. Maps will usually have a number along each edge of the page telling you which map number it

P.S. Dont forget you can always USE A SAT NAV

Lastly, DO NOT attempt to read the map *whilst* driving. This is stressful and very dangerous. Check your map *before* you leave and perhaps jot down some directions on a post-it note.

Understand the scale of the map, so you can estimate how far away something is.

Work out how to get there before you arrive. Use a system that suits you. You may have a post-it note on the page you are using, with some notes, like "Down Drake Street, first left, second right after the roundabout" Others may prefer a sketch of a map, with some main landmarks and street names drawn in.

Develop some abbreviations, that you find easy to use, but are also generic enough for others to interpret, e.g. 1st (R), 3rd (L), etc.

Section Four: Island Home

Camp out in style by becoming the consummate domestic technician.

Security
Emergency Contacts

■ Imagine being totally alone on an island. This is how some teenagers might feel when their parents go away for a few days and leave them in charge of the whole house.
Fill out this form with your folks – it will help you keep the house in tip-top condition:

Where are your parents going?
□

They will be away from:
□ (date)   to

Expected arrival time home:
□

Parents will be staying at (hotel, caravan park, friends' address):
□

Contact numbers whilst they are away (mobile numbers, hotel numbers, etc.)
□

Emergency contacts:
Name
Number
□

For real emergencies, call 999 (life threatening situations). Otherwise, contact:

Local police station (break-ins, security concerns, etc.):
□

Family doctor: (general accidents or illness)
□

NHS Direct call this number if you are feeling unwell and need advice from a nurse
□**0845 4647**

Local vet: (pet accident or illness)
□

Coastguard
□ 999 and ask for the Coastguard

Security alert:
Remember to clear the mail daily, turn the porch light on at night time, keep doors and windows locked when you leave the house and at night, and use the alarm system if there is one.

Other security instructions:
Bin collection day (most areas put bin on kerb the night before, but check local rules):
▶

Neigbourhood Watch Number

Local Police Station number
▶

Shopping

Survival Mission 5

■ If your ship was about to sink, what supplies would you take with you?
Fill out this form with your parents so that you can stock up whilst they are away.

Best shopping day: _____

Best place to shop: _____

STANDARD STOCK: Check these items before you go and add to the list if they need replacing (parents can write standard items here to be checked off to buy):

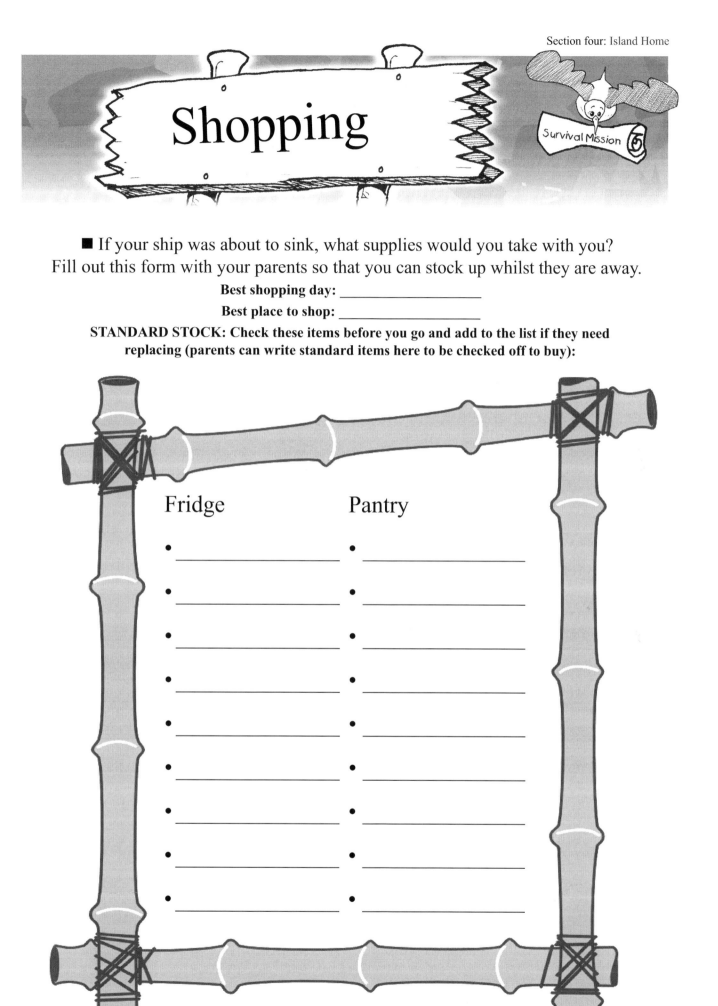

Fridge

- _____
- _____
- _____
- _____
- _____
- _____
- _____
- _____
- _____

Pantry

- _____
- _____
- _____
- _____
- _____
- _____
- _____
- _____
- _____

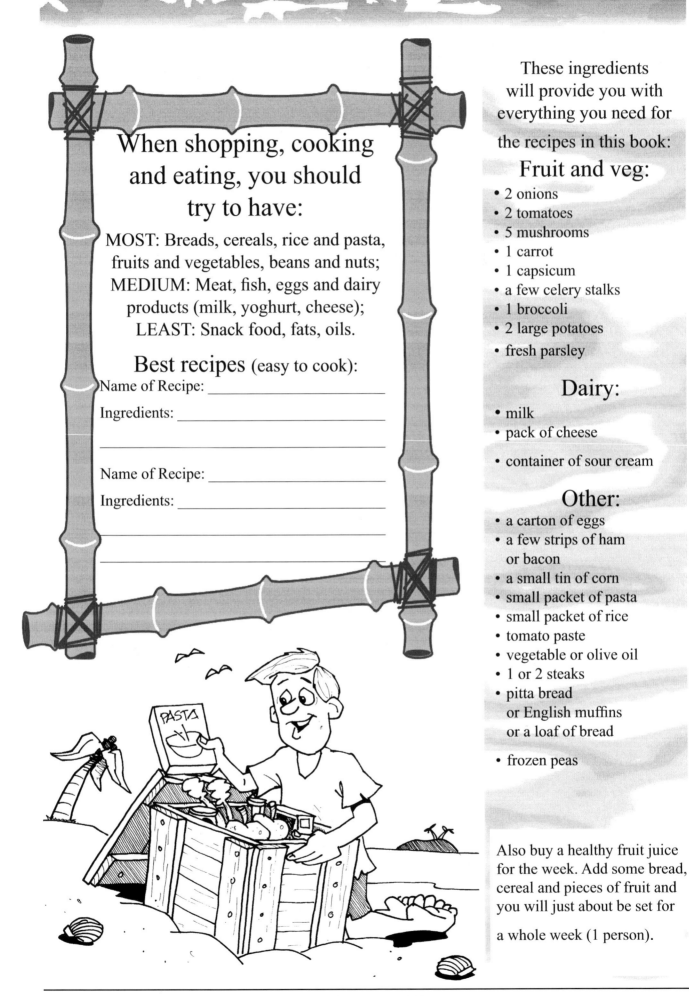

When shopping, cooking and eating, you should try to have:

MOST: Breads, cereals, rice and pasta, fruits and vegetables, beans and nuts;
MEDIUM: Meat, fish, eggs and dairy products (milk, yoghurt, cheese);
LEAST: Snack food, fats, oils.

Best recipes (easy to cook):

Name of Recipe: _____

Ingredients: _____

_____

Name of Recipe: _____

Ingredients: _____

_____

_____

These ingredients will provide you with everything you need for the recipes in this book:

Fruit and veg:
- 2 onions
- 2 tomatoes
- 5 mushrooms
- 1 carrot
- 1 capsicum
- a few celery stalks
- 1 broccoli
- 2 large potatoes
- fresh parsley

Dairy:
- milk
- pack of cheese
- container of sour cream

Other:
- a carton of eggs
- a few strips of ham or bacon
- a small tin of corn
- small packet of pasta
- small packet of rice
- tomato paste
- vegetable or olive oil
- 1 or 2 steaks
- pitta bread or English muffins or a loaf of bread
- frozen peas

Also buy a healthy fruit juice for the week. Add some bread, cereal and pieces of fruit and you will just about be set for a whole week (1 person).

Winning Recipes

NAME OF DISH: _____ HOW MANY IT SERVES: _____

INGREDIENTS (include amounts):

- _____
- _____
- _____
- _____
- _____

- _____
- _____
- _____
- _____
- _____

METHOD:

1. _____
2. _____
3. _____
4. _____
5. _____
6. _____
7. _____
8. _____

NOTE: Make sure you have included microwave or stove settings and times. DO NOT PUT METAL IN A MICROWAVE, IT CAN BE DANGEROUS

Things to remember/serving tips:

- _____
- _____
- _____

This dish goes well with: _____

How leftovers can be stored/used:

SURVIVAL: TEEN ISLAND
The ultimate survival guide for 15 - 18 year olds.

59

Cooking

Boiling an Egg

- Cover eggs in a saucepan with cold water and place on high heat.

- Bring to a simmer (the boiling does not have to be rapid, just gentle rolling bubbles is fine).

- Lower the heat a little and time for a further 3 minutes for a soft-boiled egg, 4 - 5 minutes for a medium boiled egg and 6-7 minutes for a hard-boiled egg.

- These times will vary according to the temperature of the egg when you begin, but use trial-and-error and you will find your perfect egg boiling time.

- If you want to peel the hard-boiled egg, run under cold water, tap around the edges and peel into a strainer over the running water.

DID YOU KNOW? The green film that you sometimes see around the yolk of an over-boiled egg is iron sulfide – the result of a chemical reaction between the iron in the yolk and the hydrogen sulphide in the white. Although it sounds and looks gross, it is fine to eat.

http://science.howstuffworks.com/question616.htm

Omelette

Sick of boiled eggs?

Why not get creative with an omelette?

The best omelettes are made using a non-stick pan so they do not burn or stick to the pan.

- Crack 2 eggs in a bowl.

- Add salt, pepper, parsley or chives to taste and whisk with a fork until slightly frothy.

  Now you can add a personal touch with your favourite flavour combo. Try chopped onion, tomato, mushroom or ham or get creative with some other ideas. Two tablespoons of each should be plenty.

- Gently fry these ingredients for about 2 minutes in a hot frying pan with a small amount of butter or oil.

- Pour in egg mix and let it set. Use a spatula to lift the edges as it cooks, and start to tilt the pan so the omelette slides easily.

- When it is almost cooked through, flip the omelette with the spatula. Cook for another minute or so, then slide out of the pan onto some toast, sprinkle with grated cheese and enjoy!

DID YOU KNOW? Charles Blondin, the first man to ever complete a tightrope crossing of Niagara Falls, made one crossing in 1860 in which he stopped halfway and made an omelette on a portable grill!

www.secure-bookings.co.uk/niagara-falls/area.html

SURVIVAL: TEEN ISLAND
The ultimate survival guide for 15 - 18 year olds.

61

Fried Rice

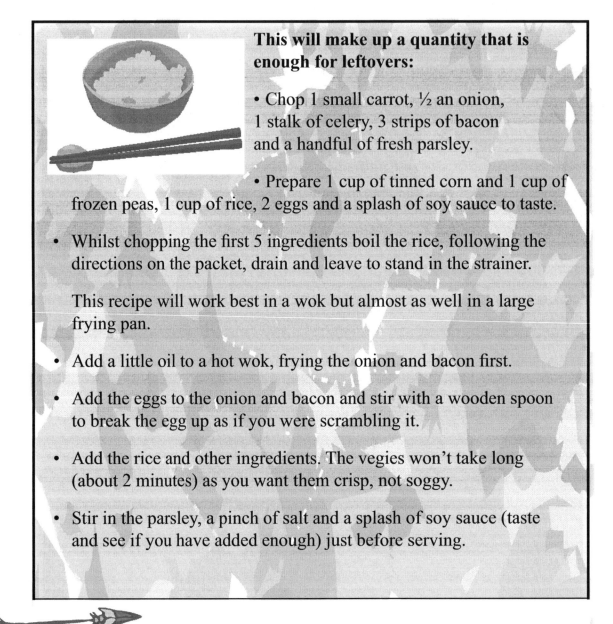

This will make up a quantity that is enough for leftovers:

• Chop 1 small carrot, ½ an onion, 1 stalk of celery, 3 strips of bacon and a handful of fresh parsley.

• Prepare 1 cup of tinned corn and 1 cup of frozen peas, 1 cup of rice, 2 eggs and a splash of soy sauce to taste.

• Whilst chopping the first 5 ingredients boil the rice, following the directions on the packet, drain and leave to stand in the strainer.

This recipe will work best in a wok but almost as well in a large frying pan.

• Add a little oil to a hot wok, frying the onion and bacon first.

• Add the eggs to the onion and bacon and stir with a wooden spoon to break the egg up as if you were scrambling it.

• Add the rice and other ingredients. The vegies won't take long (about 2 minutes) as you want them crisp, not soggy.

• Stir in the parsley, a pinch of salt and a splash of soy sauce (taste and see if you have added enough) just before serving.

WHAT DO CARS AND RICE HAVE IN COMMON?

The Japanese interpretation of Toyota is "bountiful rice field" and Honda means "main rice field". www.tipsofallsorts.com/rice.html

Pasta Dish

The beauty of this dish is that there are endless combinations of shapes and sauces. Choose from macaroni (tubes), farfalle (bows), fettucine (flat strips), spaghetti (rounded strips) or spirals, to name a few.

- For a simple pasta dish, boil any of the above to the instructions on the packet (use about ¼ of a 500g packet per person, less if you are using lots of vegies).

- Whilst boiling the pasta, chop and fry any combination of these ingredients in a frying pan with a little oil: a clove of garlic, ¼ of an onion, 1 tomato, ¼ of a capsicum, 2 – 3 small mushrooms, a handful of beans or chopped broccoli.

- To your vegie mix, add a dash of pasta sauce or tomato paste so it looks like "real" pasta sauce. You might also like to add salt, pepper and chopped parsley to taste.

- While the vegies are cooked but still firm, pour over the drained pasta and serve. For a professional touch, sprinkle some parmesan cheese on top, if you have some.

Substitute the tomato paste with a dash of cream for a different taste sensation.

DID YOU KNOW? Some pasta is coloured black or grey using squid ink!

SURVIVAL: TEEN ISLAND
The ultimate survival guide for 15 - 18 year olds.

63

Steak & Veg

If you have a stove-top and a microwave, then you should be able to make this simple and satisfying meal.

How to cook a steak:

• Use a non-stick pan and you will not need to use oil – the fat from the steak should be enough, but if you have an old, sticky pan, just use a drop the size of 20 cent coin.

• Use freshly-bought meat or steak that has been defrosted slowly in the fridge (take from the freezer the day beforehand). Only use microwave defrosting if you are familiar with the settings. Don't defrost on the bench at room temperature – it will be a field day for bacteria and hungry dogs.

• Heat the pan until it is very hot.

• Cook on one side until you see the blood coming through the top.

• Turn once and cook on the other side until you see blood coming through.

• Turn the heat down and continue cooking for a few more minutes. Test the firmness with some tongs. Rare steak will be soft, (like poking your chin) medium steak will be springy (like poking your nose) and well-done steak will be firm (like poking your forehead).

www.answerbag.com/q_view.php/385

How to microwave vegies:

• Cut vegetables into bite-sized pieces. By making them all the same size you can ensure even cooking.

• Use only microwave safe containers.

• Cover loosely with cling wrap so steam can escape.

• Add a bit of water in the container, but you don't need to cover all the vegies.

• Try 1 - 2 minutes for soft /small vegies like squash, snow peas, mushrooms.

• 3 - 4 minutes for firmer vegies like carrot, broccoli and corn on the cob.

• 4 - 5 min for each small potato or sweet potato.

• Stir or turn vegies in the middle of cooking to check progress and make sure there is enough water (if the vegies look dry, add a little more).

Footy Potato

Micro-safe: The following "microwave safe" test is best done with help from an adult to avoid any catastrophes. Test your dish for 30 seconds on high to determine if it is microwave safe. Some sources suggest putting a cup of water alongside the dish you are testing. If the dish becomes hot, don't use it. If the water is hot but the dish is cool, it should be fine to use. Many dishes are marked "microwave safe". Look for these first.

This simple, yummy snack can be enjoyed at any time – not just while watching the footy, and is another dish with many taste options.

- Take one large potato – one shaped like a football is best.

- Pierce it with a fork, then stick it in the microwave in a microwave-safe dish for about 5 minutes. Poke it again with a skewer if (you have one) or the fork, to see how well it is cooked. Turn the potato over and estimate how much longer it needs (up to another 6 minutes). If you are unsure, cook for 1 minute at a time until you think it is done.

- Use a knife to cut off the top of the spud, then gently scoop out the inside with a teaspoon, leaving a wall of potato to keep your fillings in.

- In a bowl, mash the scooped-out mix with a teaspoon of butter and a dash of milk (just enough to make it creamy), then add your fillings:

Try one of these combos or mix 'em up to create your own taste sensation:

  - Baked beans or spaghetti (use a small-sized tin);
  - Chopped chives and ½ cup sour cream;
  - Chopped ham or bacon (fry this separately and chop finely) & mushrooms;
  - Tinned tuna and grated cheese;
  - Tomato salsa and chopped broccoli.

- Fill the potato so that it is full, but not overflowing. Add fresh herbs, salt and pepper to taste. Top with grated cheese and place the top back on.

- Microwave for another 2 - 5 minutes on high or place in a preheated oven (about 180°) for approximately 10 minutes. Check to see how well it is cooking – if the potato was well cooked before it won't need as long.

- Serve with a dollop of sour cream.

DID YOU KNOW? The potato was the first vegetable to be grown in space. www.texmextogo.com/potatoes/Default.htm

SURVIVAL: TEEN ISLAND
The ultimate survival guide for 15 - 18 year olds.

65

Home-Made Pizzas

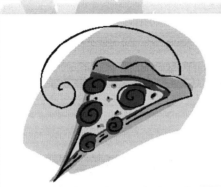

Five steps to a quick snack that is healthier and tastier than any "dial-a-pizza".

As you are getting ready, preheat your oven to 180° (big pizzas) or turn on your grill to medium-high (muffin or toast pizzas).

1. Prepare and chop your ingredients.

   You will need: Tomato paste / pasta sauce / tomato sauce, grated cheese, herbs such as parsley, oregano or basil (fresh or dried), olive oil (optional).

   Choose and chop: Ham or bacon, onion, olives, tomato, capsicum, tinned pineapple chunks, corn kernels, mushrooms, broccoli, zucchini.

   Gourmet: If you have any, add some crumbled fetta cheese, capers, asparagus, artichokes, cashews, sun-dried tomatoes.

2. Choose your base: For a meal, try pitta bread (flat bread). For a snack, use toasted English muffins, cut in half, or slices of toast.

3. Assemble the pizza: Thinly spread sauce or paste on your base and add a sprinkle of herbs. Spread a selection of toppings across the pizza. If you make sure there is only one layer of toppings then they will all cook better.

4. Top the pizza with grated cheese, a tiny drizzle of oil, salt and pepper, and place in the oven or grill on a foil-lined tray.

5. Bake for about 10 minutes and check to see if the toppings are looking done, i.e. if the cheese is melted and bubbling and the edges of the base are crispy.

Laundry

■ Unlike real survivors, you probably would not survive long wearing the same clothes every day – your friends would desert you! Every laundry appliance is different and will vary in the way it is used. Ask your parents to help you fill out this sheet:

The washing machine: different clothes require different settings, however some parents are more fussy than others.

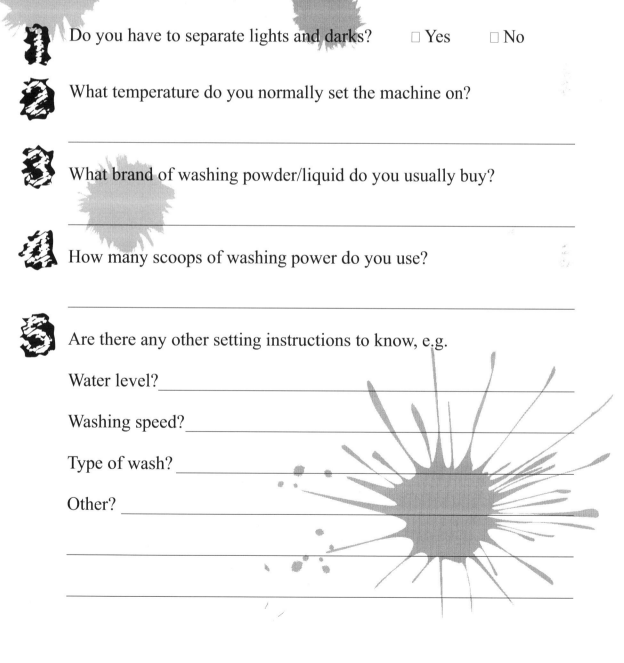

1   Do you have to separate lights and darks?   ☐ Yes   ☐ No

2   What temperature do you normally set the machine on?

_____

3   What brand of washing powder/liquid do you usually buy?

_____

4   How many scoops of washing power do you use?

_____

5   Are there any other setting instructions to know, e.g.

Water level?_____

Washing speed?_____

Type of wash? _____

Other? _____

_____

_____

Laundry Tips

- If a piece of clothing has a bad stain, wash it separately in a bucket with a bit of detergent. Do the same for any delicate fabrics.

- If you are unsure about how to wash any clothes, such as a silk top or a woollen jumper, read the clothing label and follow the washing instructions.

- When you load the clothes, make sure they are evenly spread around the machine so it is balanced. If the machine stops at any time, check the balance again.

- Do not overfill the machine as this will put it off balance or the clothes will not get washed properly. It may even cause the machine to become stuck or to overflow.

- If you are unsure about detergent amounts, read the side of the packet.

- Check all pockets before placing clothes in the wash. Tissues and leaky pens are common disasters.

- If you are unsure of what to do or the machine is doing weird things, see if you can find the machine manual.

Drying:

Drying clothes on the line will save your clothes and the environment, however if it is a wet day or you need your clothes quickly, use the dryer as follows (or read the clothing label if you are not sure, as some items will say "Do not tumble dry"):

Delicate fabrics:

Silk, stockings, lace, bathing suits, etc. should be placed on a gentle dry.

Medium fabrics:

Shirts, skirts and shorts can be placed on a medium setting.

Tough fabrics:

Towels, thick cottons and jeans can be placed on a high setting.

Stop the dryer every 10 minutes or so to check on the progress.

Safety alert:

If you are ever drying clothes in front of the heater, always place them about a metre away from the heater, and never leave them unattended. DO NOT USE THIS METHOD IF THERE ARE YOUNG CHILDREN AROUND. THEY MAY PULL THE CLOTHES ONTO THE HEATER.

☐www.essortment.com/in/Home.Cleaning/

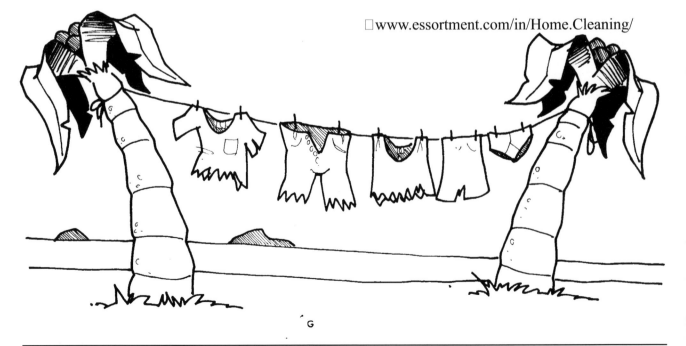

General House-Cleaning

A shabby shelter is sure to shame.
Outshine your fellow survivors by keeping your home in tip-top condition.

1. When dusting, a slightly damp cloth is better than a feather duster. The dust will cling to the rag rather than being spread around the room.

2. Vacuum your kitchen floor before mopping it. It only takes a minute to vacuum it but it will halve your mopping time.

3. On the vacuum cleaner head, the setting that looks like a brush is for lino or tiles. The one that is flat is for carpet.

4. Add floor cleaner to a bucket of water or spray cleaner onto the floor. Make sure you do a rinse mop so your floor will not resemble dried bubbles.

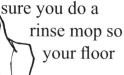

5. Always check the iron to see if it is off before you leave the room. Don't bother ironing undies, it is pretty much a waste of time. Start on a lower setting and increase for items such as cotton shirts, shorts and jeans.

6. When ironing, be careful of buttons (they can become very hot) and raised patterns on fabrics (which can melt onto the iron surface).

7. As an alternative to using a cloth that you also use to wipe the sink, use toilet paper and a spray-on bathroom cleaner to wipe the toilet seat, and then flush.

8. After scrubbing the toilet, rinse the brush by holding it inside the toilet as you flush.

9. Vinegar and newspaper make good window cleaners.

10. Only use small amounts of bathroom cleaning products, in conjunction with a sponge that you rinse regularly, or a brush with a handle.

11. Get yourself into a routine. Ask your parents what works best in your house.

Our House Routine:

☐ Write a summary here, in sequence:
(e.g. Vacuuming, Mopping, Bathrooms, Dusting, Windows)

Task: _____

Products required: _____

Instructions: _____

_____

_____

Task: _____

Products required: _____

Instructions: _____

_____

_____

Task: _____

Products required: _____

Instructions: _____

_____

_____

Task: _____

Products required: _____

Instructions: _____

_____

_____

Task: _____

Products required: _____

Instructions: _____

_____

_____

Babysitting

Survival Mission 5

A neighbouring islander has asked you to look after their young tribe. This form will help you handle them with ease.

Parents' names:

Mobile contact:

Child's name/s: Age/s:

Meals/food that they eat:

Allergies/illnesses:

Medication (including dosage):

Bed time:

Lights out:

Bed time routine:

Favourite stories/toys, etc:

Rules (TV, computer, etc):

Other things to remember:

Emergency contact name/number:

Neighbour contact name/number:

Address and nearest cross road for emergency situations if an ambulance is required:

Emergency

(police, fire, ambulance): **999** (U.K.)

NHS Direct (England and Wales) 0845 46 47

NHS24 (Scotland) 08454 242424

Europe wide Emergency Number

112

Babysitting Considerations:

 Arrive on time.

 Negotiate a fair rate before you start – either a per hour or a total amount for the whole night is fine.

Fill out the form with the parents.

 If there are very young children, ask for a quick demo on feeding, changing, bathing and putting to bed.

 Ask what is required, e.g. cooking a meal, bathing children, changing them, light cleaning tasks.

If it is a regular gig, get to know the house, such as where you can locate a first aid kit, a torch (in case of blackouts), etc.

If you are sitting during the day, take along some ideas for games or activities. Amused children make less trouble!

Find out what time the parents will be expected home.

Ask if you are expected to let the phone ring out or take a message. If you leave messages, make them very clear and in an obvious place. It is a nice idea to leave a little note thanking the family for the opportunity to baby-sit and telling them how the children behaved.

 If you have any concerns, it is better to contact the parents. A two minute phone conversation might save you a night of stress and the parents will usually see this as a sign that you are responsible and care about their children.

Be confident in expressing the negotiated amount. Work out the number of hours you have been there and calculate the amount, rounding to the nearest half hour.

How will you get there and home? It is not advisable to walk home at night or accept a ride from a parent who has been out drinking. Make other arrangements.

Don'ts:
- Don't babysit if you have a contagious illness such as a bad cold.
- Don't make long phone calls. If you have to make a call, use your mobile.
- Don't invite anyone else over, unless you have permission.
- Don't have the TV or radio up too loud when the children are sleeping.
- Don't stray from the routine explained to you. **Children will talk!**

Check websites such as: □www.urbanext.uiuc.edu/babysitting/ and □www.ci.mesa.az.us/police/literature/babysit.asp to read up more on babysitting.

Section Five:
Serious Stuff

If you feel stranded, don't sit there and stress -
signal for someone to help: S.O.S.

Twenty Ways to Beat Stress

1. Set small goals: Write down 2 – 3 achievable goals that you would like to complete in the next few hours. <u>Over</u>estimate the time you think it will take – that way you will be pleasantly surprised.

2. Learn how to prioritise – make a list of things that need to get done and number them in order of priority, then rewrite in that order. Cross things off as you do them.

3. Do you keep "putting off" doing things? Just start. This is often the hardest part.

4. Breathe: Sit comfortably in your chair, close your eyes and breathe deeply (in for 4 counts through your nose, out for 4 counts through your mouth). If you place your hand on your abdomen and focus on getting your abdomen (instead of your chest) to rise and fall as you breathe, then you will be breathing more deeply.

5. Listen to music – relaxing whilst studying and some fun, funky music as a release.

6. If you don't understand something, leave it and come back to it later. A fresh mind often works better.

7. Have frequent breaks (about every 30 minutes take 5 minutes off).

8. Take notes to read on car journeys or on public transport. This will make good use of your time.

9. You can combine work and exercise – read your study notes on the exercise bike or recite notes in your head as you swim laps.

10. Try herbal tea, such as chamomile or fruit tea instead of normal tea or coffee. Caffeine can interfere with sleep and increase the tendency to feel agitated.

11. Eat well – the more nutrients you get into your body, the more energy you will have, giving you more motivation to study and less reason to stress.

12. Don't use medication such as sleeping tablets without medical advice from your doctor. It may just end up worse.

13. Exercise, even if it is just walking the dog or cycling to school.

14. Talk to or walk your pet – pets are known to reduce stress in people.

15. Tape all your favourite TV shows during exam time so you won't get tempted by the box when you really need to be studying.

16. During exams, do the easiest, then favourite, then difficult questions.

17. Recognise when you are stressed – know the symptoms which attack you.

18. Talk to someone close to you – ask for their support in helping you with study, chores, or in providing a sympathetic ear.

19. See a counsellor/doctor/teacher if the stress is affecting your mental, emotional and/or physical health.

20. Have several plans for next year – if you keep saying "If I don't get into this course I don't know what I will do" it is putting a lot of pressure on yourself.

SURVIVAL: TEEN ISLAND
The ultimate survival guide for 15 - 18 year olds in Europe.

75

Tribal Conflict (Bullying)

Imagine an island where there are hundreds of young people, all living together. These people must learn together, socialise together and survive the challenges of island life together. But these ups and downs, instead of bringing all the islanders together, divide them into alliances. They form smaller tribes, and in these tribes they start to act, speak and dress differently. Although some of these tribes are friendly towards each other, others are involved in ongoing conflicts, where wars of words are common. Sometimes, members of one tribe might take a hostage, and submit them to the ultimate torture – bullying.

Bullying comes in many forms, such as physical violence (hitting, punching, kicking), name calling, putting down, teasing or mimicking, spreading rumours, calling verbal threats, writing nasty notes, e-mails or text messages, stealing or damaging personal belongings or simply excluding a person from group activities in or outside the classroom.

By the upper years of high school, most students start to mature and focus on issues such as study and thinking about their future lives. A lot of the bullying experienced in the first years of high school may have stopped, but this is not always the case. Some students are still singled out and picked on by others. After years of enduring cruelty from others, the self-esteem of these individuals may be so badly damaged that they have problems in their lives as adults. If you, or someone you know is experiencing bullying of any kind, then you need to do something about it. There are a few ideas on the next page.

Survival Kit

– For Tribal Conflict (Bullying)

☐ Firstly, know and believe the reasons why people tease others. If you keep these reasons in mind, it can help you to realise that bullying is usually more about the other person's problems than yours. See bullying as a weakness, not a strength.

☐ Bullies are often feeling insecure themselves and put others down as a self-defence mechanism. These people are often bullied themselves in other areas of their lives, like in their home, by their family. Others are just on a big power trip and think that if they are a bully, then they will look cool and others will be threatened by them, so they basically get their own way. Some people bully because their friends are doing it and they are just behaving like sheep, afraid to do anything differently.

☐ Don't be fooled into thinking that everyone likes people who bully. Many people who tease others and seem popular are often seen as intimidating and are not really respected by others – it's just that nobody has bothered standing up to them.

☐ Sometimes bullies are people who are just not good at accepting and tolerating those who are different.

You have probably heard this a million times, but one of the best ways to stop bullying is to pretend it doesn't get to you. This might not work straight away but sooner or later the person hassling you will get bored. The "reward" that bullies get is often the nervous, angry or upset reaction from their victims. If you don't satisfy them with this reward, then their power trip will not work.

It is a good idea to find that balance between remaining true to yourself, whilst toning down certain behaviours so that you don't provoke them. For example, if they are hassling you for always being the first one with your hand up in class, perhaps you could think about giving other classmates a go in answering questions.

SURVIVAL: TEEN ISLAND
The ultimate survival guide for 15 - 18 year olds .

77

Survival Kit

– For Tribal Conflict (Bullying)

☐ Talk to a friend about it. Knowing that you are not alone and that you are liked and valued by others can help you to ignore the pathetic opinions of the perpetrators.

☐ Tell an adult whom you trust, such as a parent, teacher or counsellor. They may be able to offer some good advice for your specific situation, or they may have the ability to intervene if the situation is really bad.

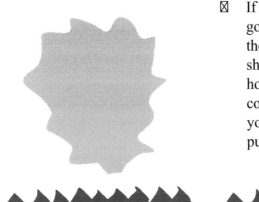

☐ Let your teachers know so that they can keep an eye out for it. You might have some ideas for how they can deal with the problem, such as devising a seating plan or changing the way they give group tasks to the class. On a wider scale, make anonymous suggestions to support or improve your school's bullying policy.

☒ If you feel really threatened, go to a safe place, such as the library at school or a shopping centre on the way home. Many bullies are cowards and will not hassle you if you are in a really public area.

☐ If the bullying is affecting your feelings of safety or happiness on a regular basis, ask the school counsellor or a trusted teacher if they can help locate a good counselling service. Alternatively, speak to your family doctor or church leader, who may also be able to offer advice on where to seek counselling.

call Childline 08001111 for help and advice at any time.

also see www.donthideit.com
www.there4me.com
www.worriedneed2talk.org.uk/
www.kidscape.org.uk
www.britkid.org.uk

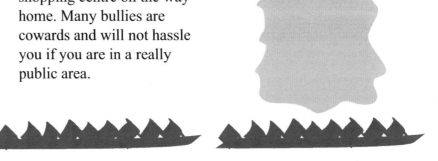

A Barrel of Rum Fer Me Hearties

Centuries ago, when sailors were exploring the islands of the worlds, alcoholic beverages were very important because the alcohol preserved the drink for longer than if it was plain water. Rations of beer were given to sailors instead of stale water, which made the sailors sick. Nowadays, the opposite is true, and people are encouraged to drink water so that alcohol does not make them sick!

The best way to prevent drug and alcohol related problems is to be aware of the facts so that you can make informed choices.

Alcohol and other drugs are a part of our society and are readily available, so it is up to the individual to make choices that will hopefully preserve their health, safety and dignity. The unpleasant physical and social side effects of drug abuse are well-known, but even one night of binge drinking can be enough to cause conflicts, regrets or embarrassing situations.

Not drinking alcohol is not a weakness, it is a strength, it shows strength of character.

SURVIVAL: TEEN ISLAND
The ultimate survival guide for 15 - 18 year olds .

79

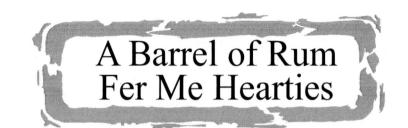

A Barrel of Rum Fer Me Hearties

The Goss

File Edit View Insert Format Tools Message Help

Send | Cut | Copy | Paste | Undo | Check | Spelling | Attach | Priority | Sign | Encrypt | Offline

From: susanne@oldschool.co.uk

To: fiona@newschool.co.uk

Cc:

Subject: The Goss

Arial | 10 | B I U A | lists | align | — |

Dear Fiona

hows your new school? We miss u here. have to tell u about joel's party. it was such a weird nite. Joel's parents were away so everyone basically got tanked. I probably would have as well but I was still getting over the flu and felt a bit rank. Wore my new boots and black skirt. Anyway simon was already there and probably had drunk about 6 beers. He paid me so much more attention than usual and kept asking me if I wanted a drink. After a while it got a bit annoying actually but at least he wanted to hang out.

He started drinking bourbon and after that he was full on. Pretty much started to grope me and at first I was ok with it so I went with him into his brother's room. Big mistake. He was trying to kiss me but it was so gross...he just stuck his tongue down my throat and was pushing down on my shoulders to hold himself up. And then he started playing with my bra strap which he thought was funny but it kind of hurt. Anyway he starts rambling about his football game and then suddenly he sits down and says he feels sick. I tried to get him outside but he just lay on the ground going "no, leave me here, I want to sleep" and then he gets up and throws up on my boots and all over the carpet. It was so gross. It was like he didn't even care or try to stop himself. After he puked he just wanted to lie there and there was no way I could move him.

Jess and paul were outside so I went and told them but they were pretty wasted and just thought it was funny. Had to wash my boots in the bath. I went back to see simon and he had thrown up again, all over himself, and then passed out. Very nice. Joel's brother came home and got so angry and he dragged simon out onto the lawn and left him there and made jess and paul clean up the spew. I stayed at katie's place down the road and in the morning we walked down and simon was still there, passed out on the lawn, looking sooo attractive. We decided to squirt him with the hose and he woke up, didn't have a clue where he was. He didn't remember anything and pretty much tried to deny what I told him.

I have decided not to go to the ball with him cos he never apologised about my boots and every time I look at him I keep getting this image of him throwing up. Everyone else thinks the whole thing was funny and we all call him "spewmon". The guys all think he's cool but none of the girls would go out with him after what I have told them.

Hope u are going well. Write and tell me all the goss.
Love Susanne

Edit | Source | Preview

80

SURVIVAL: TEEN ISLAND
The ultimate survival guide for 15 - 18 year olds in Europe.

Alcohol and Other Drugs

■ You have most probably been exposed to a lot of information about drugs at health education classes at school. Here is a quick refresher course:

Alcohol, when abused, can result in slurred speech, nausea, hangovers, loss of muscle control and loss of inhibitions in the short term (i.e. the risk of doing dangerous, embarrassing or regrettable things is increased). Long-term results of excessive drinking include brain damage, memory loss, liver cirrhosis, male impotence, shrinkage of the testicles, reduced sperm count and increased risk of menstrual problems.

Driving under the influence of alcohol is illegal because you might end up **killing yourself or someone else.** The worst thing about driving under the influence is not just that you can get caught, but that your reflexes are diminished and you could wind up in an accident – writing off your car, and as we have already said, risking injury or death for yourself, your friends and other drivers on the road (who, by the way, don't have much of a say in it). Imagine living the rest of your life with the memory of a serious car crash on your conscience.

Another problem linked to alcohol is drink spiking,

which can take place at pubs, clubs, parties or other events where alcoholic beverages (or even soft drinks) are consumed. Drugs are inconspicuously added to drinks to make the drinker, male or female, feel uninhibited, drowsy or dizzy, lose their memory or even lose consciousness. In this state, if left alone, the victim can be taken advantage of, with a high risk of sexual assault.

To avoid drink spiking, make sure you always hold or watch your drink, never leave it unattended, do not share or taste drinks with people you do not know, and do not let a stranger buy you a drink, especially if you do not see it being poured.

Do not drink something if it looks tampered with or tastes strange – let another person know if you think your drink has been spiked. Stick together with friends, and if one of them begins acting strangely, tell a trusted adult or get them to a hospital if you are really concerned.

SURVIVAL: TEEN ISLAND
The ultimate survival guide for 15 - 18 year olds .

81

Cannabis or **Marijuana**, smoked through joints, pipes or bongs, or eaten in cookies and cakes, has the short-term effects of impaired perception, concentration, balance and reflexes. It increases heart rate and appetite – so junk food is often gorged on (not good for weight-watchers). It can produce a feeling of well-being but in higher doses this can change to hallucinations, panic attacks, confusion and paranoia. **Cannabis** is believed to trigger schizophrenia for those that are predisposed to it. It can also affect memory and concentration in the long term. Like **cigarette smoking**, the risk of respiratory problems such as cancers, emphysema, and bronchitis are increased as there are often less filters and smokers hold the substances in their lungs longer. The plastic of PVC from "bottle bongs" can also release toxic chemicals into the lungs.

The laws on **cannabis** possession and use involve fines and/or compulsory drug education sessions.

Check □http://www.knowcann uk/

Cocaine is a stimulant, which means it stimulates the central nervous system. It can produce hallucinations, convulsions and feelings like insects are crawling under the skin, or even worse, burst blood vessels in the brain. **Cocaine** is snorted, injected or smoked.

One of the problems with **cocaine** is that it  can be mixed with other substances like baking soda, sugar or talcum powder when it is sold, and this can increase unpleasant side

Ecstasy is one of the more common drugs taken at parties or nightclubs. It can produce the effect of stimulants and hallucinogens (increasing the activity of body systems and producing a distortion of perception) and is usually taken in the form of a small pill. Although taken to induce a feeling of energy and euphoria, unpleasant side effects such as nausea, jaw grinding and anxiety can also be experienced. Due to the sleeplessness and increased activity of the person taking ecstasy, the "coming down" phase can include feelings of physical exhaustion, as well as depression and irritability. Another problem with ecstasy is the inability of the body to regulate temperature. This means that the person may overheat and faint, or drink excessive amounts of water.

Speed (amphetamines) speeds up the messages between the brain and the ...ly. Amphetamines can be in the form ...powder, tablets, liquid, capsules or ...rystals and can be swallowed, snorted, injected or smoked. These drugs are taken to reduce fatigue or to induce a "high". Speed increases heart rate ...d breathing. Users can feel wide-...ke, become more talkative, excited or restless. Amphetamines can also cause irritability, anxiousness and panic attacks. Overdosing can be a problem due to the unknown strength of each batch and can result in stroke, heart failure or seizures.

Survival Kit
– Alcohol and other Drugs

■ Remember, with drugs, there is never any guarantee and even if you take every precaution, you are still putting yourself at risk.

☐ You might think you know where something comes from, but with drugs, it is always very difficult to determine the exact content and strength, not to mention the variation of effects it will have between individuals.

☐ Even somewhere that seems like a "safe environment", like someone's home, can become unsafe if everyone is "wasted".

In the case of an emergency, the apparent safest place may still be too far away from the closest ambulance.

☐ Taking drugs can become more dangerous if consumed on an empty stomach, or if mixed with other drugs. It is hard to know what may make a dangerous cocktail.

☐ Even people who think "I will just have a small amount and wait to see what happens", may have their perception warped or become easily swayed into taking more of the drug.

☐ Some people who take drugs and begin to feel unwell may be so "out of it" that they can't tell their friends about their state. Even if they do, their friends may be too scared to call an ambulance, despite the fact that an ambulance service's first priority is to assist, not call the police.

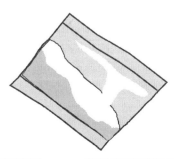

To find out more about the risks involved with taking drugs, check out these sites:

☐http://www.thesite.org/

☐http://www.youth2youth.co.uk

☐http://www.ypsh.net

☐http://www.talktofrank.com

☐http://www.adviceguide.org.uk

If you have any questions or concerns, call the Alcohol and Drug Information Service:

Wales: DAN 24/7 Wales Drug and Alcohol Helpline 0800 6 33 55 88

Addaction UK - a leading UK charity working solely in the field of drug and alcohol treatment

Tel: 0207 2515860

Alcoholics Anonymous

Tel: 0845 769 7555 (national),

Alcoline - Alcohol Problems Advisory Service (apas)

Tel: 0845 762 6316

Al-Anon Helpline 0207 4030888 10am-10pm daily (national)

Family Groups - support for family and friends

Alateen - support for young people, 12-20 years, affected by a problem drinker

Detox Support Project - residential support for people who are detoxing

Tel: (01273) 604245

Recovery Project - residential long-term treatment for people who want to address drug and/or alcohol issues

Tel: (01273) 684741

Drinkline - Helpline 0800 917 8282 (national) 9am-11pm, Monday to Friday

Drugsline

Freephone Crisis & Support Line 0808 1606606

Families Anonymous - for people affected by someone else's drug use.

Helpline 0845 1200 660

NHS Direct Tel: 0845 4647

for more addresses
see www.studymates.co.uk

SURVIVAL: TEEN ISLAND
The ultimate survival guide for 15 - 18 year olds .

83

Island Rations

When people are left to survive on an island, they are faced with the challenge of finding enough food to live on. They might have some supplies, but much of their diet will come from catching fish and searching for food in their environment. After a while, the lack of proper nutrition can take its toll. Islanders may start to lose a lot of weight and begin to look scrawny and skeletal. They may complain of hunger pains, feeling cold due to lack of energy from nutrients and suffering the effects of physical exhaustion and emotional anguish as the feeling of starvation overwhelms them.

Why would anyone choose to feel hungry when food is readily available? For those who have an eating disorder, this is the choice that they make every day.

About Amelia

A few weeks ago in Health Education class we learned about eating disorders. It made me think about Amelia. As I read through the symptoms I could relate a lot of them to they way she looks and acts.

Anorexia Nervosa

Anorexia Nervosa is characterised by extreme restrictions on food intake combined with an unhealthy body weight (significantly below the normal range).

Amelia used to be the best looking girl in our year. She was the first one to get curves and all the guys were after her. But after the Christmas holidays, she came back to school looking really skinny – well, more like skeletal actually. Her arms looked like sticks and you could see her hip bones poking through her skirt.

The person with anorexia has intense fears of gaining weight and/or losing control of their eating habits.

Amelia has always been "on a diet", but lately she has become a bit obsessed. She brings the tiniest amount of food to school each day and always looks up this little book, which tells you the calories in everything. She thinks if she eats anything we make in home economics, she will gain about 10 kilos. I didn't realise how terrified she was about gaining weight until her party last week. She wouldn't eat her own birthday cake, and then she got all narky at Lucy who poured her a drink that wasn't a "diet" drink.

> Often, the person's body image is distorted and he/she does not recognise that they are underweight.

We keep telling Amelia that she is getting too thin, but she gets kind of mad at us, and says, "Don't lie to me. I'm fat. I'm huge. Look at my legs". We look at her legs, which are like bones with skin attached, and can't understand how she can possibly call that fat

> It is often difficult to pinpoint a single cause of an eating disorder, with many factors appearing to play a role in most cases. Some examples of these factors include an extreme reaction to social expectations of thinness, family attitudes and poor communication habits, biological dysfunction, personal beliefs, anxious or submissive personality traits and/or tragic or stressful life events. People with anorexia often display an extremely low self-esteem.

Amelia's mum is tiny. She used to be a model when she was younger and has pushed Amelia into beauty contests since she was a baby. Ever since I have known Amelia she has had a magazine in her hand, and is always looking at the models, saying how fat she is compared to them. She doesn't see that she is actually way thinner than most of them. Once, Amelia told me a secret. She said that her dad once had an affair when her mum found it hard to lose weight after being pregnant. Amelia thinks it is her fault for being born – she was the one who made her mum fat and caused the affair.

Amelia has always been pretty highly strung. She goes to gymnastics three times a week and studies for hours after school. If she misses a training session or gets anything less than an A, she ends up in tears. Once, I saw her in the bathroom. She was looking at herself in the mirror, saying "I hate you, you fat cow." I remember this was after she got a low score in her maths test – but that was only because she had been off sick for a week with the flu.

> Eating disorders can damage the body and its systems, including physiological effects such as temperature sensitivity, poor bone density, fertility interference, changes in hair, skin and nails, weakness in cardiovascular system and muscles; and psychological effects such as anxiety, depression and personality changes.

SURVIVAL: TEEN ISLAND
The ultimate survival guide for 15 - 18 year olds in Europe.

85

Amelia wears baggy jumpers to school now, even on hot days. They hang off her arms but they don't really hide how thin she is. She doesn't even wear a bra anymore because she doesn't need one. I have noticed that her arms have this strange soft white hair on them, but the hair on her head is not glossy anymore. It is dull and looks thinner than it used to. When we moan about how annoying periods are, she goes really quiet, like she hasn't even got hers yet.

When we do sport, Amelia gets tired really easily. She tries to keep up but she can't run like she used to, and she often goes and hangs out in the library after phys. ed. I don't know how she copes with her gym classes after school.

It's hard to talk to Amelia these days. She used to be a lot of fun but now all she ever talks about is food and her weight. She is also way more moody and snappy and at other times she just zones out completely. I didn't really know what to do about all of this. I have decided just to be really nice to Amelia all the time so she can trust me and maybe if she needs to, she can talk.

Many specialised organisations and support groups exist to assist in the physical and psychological healing of people with eating disorders. Ongoing counselling to restore a healthy perception of self, and careful monitoring of an adequate diet, may need to continue for months or even years. Many people "recover" from eating disorders and go on to live a normal, healthy life, although others are at risk of relapse during stressful periods of their life.

One month later – The other day, Amelia told me that she is seeing a counsellor. She didn't say why but I am pretty sure it is about her eating problems. I really hope they are helping her.

Two months later – Today I saw Amelia eat a muesli bar. She saw me looking at her and she said "Do you think this will make me fat?" I said "No, I think it will be healthy for you." She kind of thought for a while and nodded. I think she might be getting better.

Three months later – Amelia told me her secret today. She does have anorexia, and she has been getting counselling for a few months now. I think it was really hard for her to tell me but I am glad that she did. She said that she has good days and bad days, but she is lucky to have been caught in the early stages. We had lunch together. Today, she ate it all.

Sources: see Page 87 for recommended websites.

Survival Kit
For Island Rations

■ **You might have concerns about your own eating habits or know someone that you are worried about.**

If you are concerned about how much you think about food and your weight, then you may have a problem. If others comment about your weight loss or behaviour, remember that they are not trying to attack you, they are approaching you out of genuine concern. Tell someone you trust about your worries and allow them to help you. If you act now, you may save yourself from devastating effects later down the track.

If you have concerns about a family member or a friend, keep in mind that many people who have eating disorders may respond with anger or denial. Supporting them with patience and acceptance will help. Give them opportunities to talk, be honest with them and do not be critical of their behaviour. Encourage them when they are trying to do something to address the problem.

Finally, remember that the various eating disorders, such as bulimia and anorexia, can be quite complex and require professional help. There are many support organisations for people with eating disorders throughout Europe. The numbers below are a possible starting point, or contact your local doctor or hospital for more information.

Sources

- Beating Eating Disorders www.b-eat.co.uk/
- BBC - Health - Conditions - Eating disorders ☐www.bbc.co.uk/health/conditions/mental_health/disorders_eating.shtm
- National Centre For Eating Disorders - effective treatment for all ... www.eating-disorders.org.uk/

  Eating Disorders

  •www.rcpsych.ac.uk/mentalhealthinformation/mentalhealthproblems/eatingdisorders.aspx

  ☐www.nice.org.u
- www.eatingdisorderexpert.co.uk/
- www.something-fishy.org/
- For good diet information see **The Eat well, stay slim, Budget Cookbook, Joanna McIllhatton Aber Publishing**

SURVIVAL: TEEN ISLAND
The ultimate survival guide for 15 - 18 year olds .

87

Trouble In Paradise

Imagine a young girl who has been living on her island for some time now. She is happy, successful and loves to party with all the other islanders. Life is good. Sometimes, she is reminded about the things that can go wrong, but she thinks, "They won't happen to me" and for quite a while, they don't. Then, without warning, a tiny speck becomes visible on the horizon. It's coming her way. A new arrival invading her blissful paradise. And she knows that the new arrival will change her whole life on the island, for a very long time. Will she stay and welcome this new arrival? It's a scary thought. She knows her alternatives, but is not sure which one to take. She looks away, hoping that it isn't real, but when she looks back, it is still there, getting closer and closer. She knows that she has to accept this reality and make a decision.

Teenage pregnancy

is a real issue, and despite all the facts, many young people think it will never happen to them and take risks with their behaviour. Not having available protection, getting "caught up in the moment", or not knowing the facts such as the pill possibly failing after forgetting just one dose – are just some of the reasons why teenagers do get pregnant. But however frightening it might seem, there are many support services available that can help young people make the choice that is right for them, and to know that they are not alone.

It is important that young females and males know all the options available for safe sex, emergency contraception and services for unplanned pregnancies.

Calling Mel

The phone rings at Melanie's house. It is 10 pm.

Melanie:	Hello?
Belinda:	Hi, Melanie? Sorry to call so late. I need to talk to someone.
Melanie:	That's OK. What's wrong?
Belinda:	Oh, I just don't know what to do. I think ... I think there's something wrong.
Melanie:	Like what? Are you hurt, or sick?
Belinda:	No. I think ... I think I might be pregnant.
Melanie:	Oh, my god. Are you serious? I mean, do you know for sure?
Belinda:	Well, no, but I am late with my period and I'm never late. And I have felt sick for the last few days. Oh, what am I going to do? This is going to ruin my life.
Melanie:	Is it Hamish, I mean, do you think he's ... ?
Belinda:	Yeah. Oh, Mel. We just didn't think, I mean not until it was too late. And then I kind of just hoped it would be OK. I totally deserve this for being so stupid.
Melanie:	Hey, look. Nobody deserves things like this. I mean, I think the first thing you need to do is find out if you really are pregnant.
Belinda:	I can't. I'm too scared. I just want it to go away.
Melanie:	I know. But the sooner you find out, the more time you have to make a decision.
Belinda:	What do I do? I can't go to our doctor and I don't trust those home test things.
Melanie:	Well, I've heard the home tests are pretty reliable, actually. Look, you know what? There's this place in the city, Family Planning or something. My cousin went there when she was 16 and they have teenagers come in all the time. I can go with you, if you like.
Belinda:	Yeah, I guess. Thanks. Mel, I don't know what'll happen if I am pregnant. Hamish is going to freak out, I will have to leave home. I just ... I just hate myself for being so stupid.
Melanie:	Belinda, you are not the first person this has happened to. Stop being so hard on yourself. Look, these people deal with heaps of girls our age. They will know how to help you. Try not to worry until you go and see them. And your parents – well, they might be more supportive than you think. They love you and will realise that you didn't do this to get at them. Look, I will come over at 9 am tomorrow. We will catch a bus in – I don't think you even need to make an appointment. My cousin said they are really nice and they will give you all the help you need.
Belinda:	OK, 9 tomorrow. Thanks, Mel, I didn't know who else to call, but I'm glad you are here. See you tomorrow. Bye.

SURVIVAL: TEEN ISLAND
The ultimate survival guide for 15 - 18 year olds in Europe.

89

Pregnancy Things to Know

Pregnancy is not predictable. Fertilisation can occur at any stage in a woman's cycle and some of the methods of protection that might seem OK may in fact be quite unreliable. Many young people who "slip up" just cross their fingers and hope it will be alright – sometimes it is, but sometimes it isn't.

The way a **pregnancy** is measured is from the first day of a woman's last period. For example, if you started your last period on May 6, and you missed the next one, due in early June, then you would be considered 5 weeks pregnant on June 10. Sometimes it is difficult to tell exactly how far along in the pregnancy a woman is, especially if she has had frequent unprotected sex.

Other than missing a period, other symptoms of **pregnancy** include bloating, nausea, tender breasts and increased urination. These can all be symptoms for other things, so one way to get a quick and confidential confirmation is by a home **pregnancy** test, which are quite accurate these days. The best way to be sure is to visit a doctor or Family Planning clinic, as they can not only give you an accurate result and check your general health, they can also provide important counselling and advice.

So what happens if a young woman is

pregnant? There are several options, including the ones outlined below. It is important to consider each one after looking at all the facts and thinking about what will be the best outcome. Having the support of parents or another trusted adult will make this process easier.

Many women choose to **keep the baby**, especially if they have a supportive network of family and friends and/or a partner who is willing to become involved and provide support. Some women choose to have the baby and then place the child up for **adoption**. This arrangement is a legally binding agreement where the legal rights of parenting the child are passed on to the adoptive parents. Because of the increase in support and services for women who wish to continue their pregnancy and have the child, and also increased access to support and counselling for the process of a pregnancy termination, **adoption** has become less common, but it can still be done.

Most women have **abortions** around their 6th or 7th week of pregnancy. The **termination** involves a medical procedure – removing the pregnancy by gentle suction, which is safe, simple and low risk. The process becomes more complex after 12 weeks. The process takes only 10-15 minutes but the woman usually spends a

SURVIVAL: TEEN ISLAND
The ultimate survival guide for 15 - 18 year olds.

few hours at the clinic, recovering. Most abortions are performed under a light general anaesthetic. There may be some bleeding and cramping after the procedure, which is common. It is advisable to have someone drive the woman to and from the procedure.

The abortion laws in the U.K apply to Wales, Scotland and England but *NOT to Northern Ireland.* Providing that two doctors confirm that her need for an abortion fits the legal criteria, a woman does not need the consent of her own doctor, her partner or her family to have an abortion.

Women under 16 can have an abortion, without parental consent in some circumstances. Despite legal time limits 87% of abortions take place within the first 12 weeks of pregnancy. In may be difficult to access abortion after 12 weeks.

Most abortions are carried out when two doctors agree that the risk to a woman's mental or physical health or the health of her existing child(ren) would be at greater risk if she were to continue with the pregnancy.

The most ideal situation is if pregnancy is prevented in the first place.

Here is a quick guide to the alternatives:

A question that some people still ask is "can a woman get pregnant if she has sex for the first time?" In short, the answer is YES. Protection needs to be used even from the first time if you want any kind of guarantee that you will not get pregnant.

One of the most common forms of protection, which will also provide Sexually Transmitted Infection (STI) protection, is the faithful condom. Condoms can be purchased almost anywhere these days – chemists, supermarkets or petrol stations are a few venues. Even if a girl has not started her periods she can still ovulate at any time and become pregnant, so condoms are recommended.

SURVIVAL: TEEN ISLAND
The ultimate survival guide for 15 - 18 year olds in Europe.

91

Things to know

The process of seeking the **pill** as a form of contraception can seem quite daunting, but many girls find that telling their mum, or another trusted adult, is easier than they thought, and many parents will be supportive of their daughter choosing to be responsible about **sex**.

FASTFAX The pill is one of the most effective and safe forms of contraceptive benefiting millions of women ove the years.

The pill is free

6136 67473 3

1 JOHN G HEALTH
2 SARAH L HEALTH
3 ALISON R HEALTH

There are 14 methods of contraception available.

* male condom

* female condom

* combined pill

* progestogen only pill

* contraceptive injection

* contraceptive patch

* implant

* intrauterine device (IUD)

* intrauterine system (IUS)

* diaphragm with spermicide

* cap with spermicide

* female sterilisation

* male sterilisation (vasectomy)

* natural family planning

You can get contraception free from your GP. Your GP is not allowed to tell your parents, it is confidential.

When using condoms make sure they have the BSI Kitemark and/or the CE Kitemark. This is a measure of quality.

If a condom breaks, see a GP asap, you may need emergency contraception to reduce the risk of pregnancy.

You may also need treatment for STDs, (sexually transmitted diseases) again your GP must treat this in confidence.

For more info, see the Brook

Advisory Website

www.brook.org.uk

Survival Kit

■ Below are some contacts, which provide support and information for the prevention and management of unplanned pregnancy:

▶ www.fpa.org.uk Family Planning

▶ http://www.careconfidential.com/London_Islington/Default.

Discovering you are unexpectedly pregnant can be a confusing and frightening experience. At Choices you will find someone you can trust to be caring and understanding, someone who will listen and offer support, someone who will not pressurise but provide information, answer your questions and help you to explore your options before making your own decision.

•www.youthinformation.com, the information toolkit for young people.

http://www.ruthinking.co.uk, fantastic site for young people, check it out and get informed.

http://www.likeitis.org.uk/, does what it says, tells it like it is. Gr8 for info and challenges some misconceptions. We really liked the locker room.

www.brook.org.uk, fantastic advice for young people, we really liked the video by young people for young people. This, and the sperm catcher game, really is worth your time.

http://www.ypsh.net/, Young People's sexual health, lots of stuff. Welcome to the all new Young People's Sexual Health Website. In here you will find open and frank info on Sexual Health, Support, Services, Contraception, Emergency Contraception and a whole lot more. Suffolk based.

http://www.tiscali.co.uk/lifestyle/healthfitness/health_advice/, well done Tiscali, this site is stuffed full of info

http://www.youthinformation.com Youthinformation.com is The National Youth Agency's online information toolkit for young people and all those working with them.

http://www.teenagehealthfreak.org/ good info by a proper doctor who knows what she is talking about. Lots of stuff including stuff on big and small willies

http://www.condomessentialwear.co.uk, need we say more?

http://www.sexetc.org/ Sex etc , sex education for teens by teens. (US site)

http://www.avert.org/yngindx.htm check out the teens pages

www.teenwire.com , another US site so it has articles in Spanish as well as English.. The true story of Becky Bell should make you think. Also some really good stuff for lesbian, gay and transgender people.

http://www.iwannaknow.org yet another American site, (well it doesnt make you a bad person), check out the differences between sex and love.

http://gayteens.about.com/, does exactly what it says

Most adults agree that the best sexual experience comes when when it is the natural part of a loving relationship.

SURVIVAL: TEEN ISLAND
The ultimate survival guide for 15 - 18 year olds in Europe.

93

Sex Smart

What would safe sex be like if you were living on a desert island? Perhaps you might have to get creative and use local resources: did you know that some early condoms were made from linen and others made of sheep intestines? Maybe you would need to use traditional treatments for sexually transmissible infections (STIs). For example, one early way of treating syphilis was to use leeches to suck the infected blood out of the area, so consider yourself lucky if your island is infested with these slippery little suckers! Of course, if you were stranded alone, then the practice of safe sex would become quite easy!

Fortunately, we now have a wealth of information and resources available to provide pregnancy protection and stave off STIs. Find out how much you know by taking this quick and painless test below:

1 If you miss your period, then you are definitely pregnant.

☐ True　　　　　　　　☐ False

2 You need parental permission to go on the pill if you are under 18 years of age.

☐ True　　　　　　　　☐ False

3 Females need to start having a pap smear ...

a. When they turn 18

b. One or two years after becoming sexually active

c. Only if they have a family history of cervical cancer

d. a or b, whichever comes first

4 Most effective for prevention of pregnancy is ...

a. Condoms

b. The pill

c. Jumping up and down after sex

d. The rhythm method

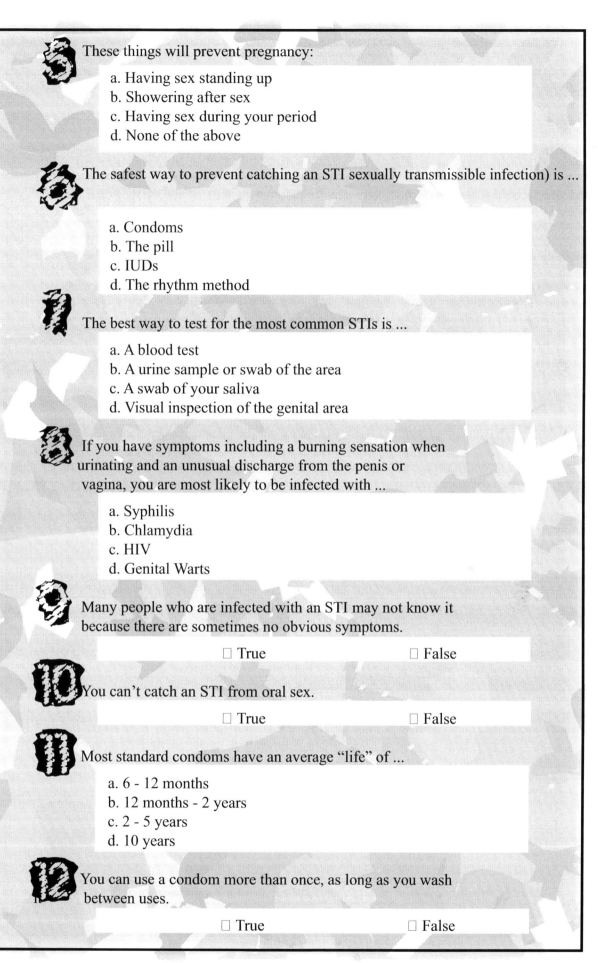

These things will prevent pregnancy:

a. Having sex standing up
b. Showering after sex
c. Having sex during your period
d. None of the above

The safest way to prevent catching an STI sexually transmissible infection) is ...

a. Condoms
b. The pill
c. IUDs
d. The rhythm method

The best way to test for the most common STIs is ...

a. A blood test
b. A urine sample or swab of the area
c. A swab of your saliva
d. Visual inspection of the genital area

If you have symptoms including a burning sensation when urinating and an unusual discharge from the penis or vagina, you are most likely to be infected with ...

a. Syphilis
b. Chlamydia
c. HIV
d. Genital Warts

Many people who are infected with an STI may not know it because there are sometimes no obvious symptoms.

☐ True   ☐ False

You can't catch an STI from oral sex.

☐ True   ☐ False

Most standard condoms have an average "life" of ...

a. 6 - 12 months
b. 12 months - 2 years
c. 2 - 5 years
d. 10 years

You can use a condom more than once, as long as you wash between uses.

☐ True   ☐ False

SURVIVAL: TEEN ISLAND
The ultimate survival guide for 15 - 18 year olds in Europe.

95

Answers

False. There are other reasons why females miss their period. Some girls have irregular cycles, particularly in the first few years of menstruation. Taking the pill can also have an effect on the cycle, especially when first starting. Poor diet or excessive dieting can also play a role in disrupting the menstrual cycle. Despite this, it is advisable that females who miss a period and have any concerns should see a doctor, as many of the other reasons may also require medical attention.

False. You can go to the doctor yourself and obtain a prescription for the pill. Read the notes for further information.

d: It is recommended for a woman to start having regular (every two years) pap smear tests at the age of 18, or after she becomes sexually active (whichever comes first), no longer than two years after the first time of having sexual intercourse and preferably sooner.

b. If taken correctly, the pill offers about 99% protection from pregnancy. Condoms used properly provide about 95 - 97% protection, and the rhythm method (having sex when a woman thinks she is not ovulating) is extremely unreliable. Jumping up and down won't work either – sperm are pretty good at swimming against gravity, no matter how much you try and assist it.

d. Don't believe the old wives' tales. All of these are not good at protecting against pregnancy. Many girls have irregular cycles and sperm can stay alive for up to five days in the uterus, and if an egg is there for the taking, it only takes one sperm to do the deed. With 200 - 500 million of the little guys in just one ejaculation, the chances of one of them being a champion swimmer are pretty reasonable!

a. Condoms are the best way to guard against STIs. The others are intended for protection against pregnancy only. Even with condoms, there is a chance of contracting an infection if infected areas on the skin are not covered by the condom and make contact with the person's partner. The best way to safeguard against this is if both parties agree to have an STI screening before starting a sexual relationship. Knowing your partner's sexual history and remaining faithful to your partner in the relationship will also enable a safer sex life.

b. A simple urine test or swab of the area will detect most STIs, except Syphilis, Hepatitis and HIV, which require a blood test.

b. Other symptoms of Chlamydia may include painful sex with possible bleeding, vaginal itching and soreness, and lower abdominal pain (women) and itching inside

96

SURVIVAL: TEEN ISLAND
The ultimate survival guide for 15 - 18 year olds.

the urethra, pain in testicles or rectum and pain with ejaculation with men.

True. If you have had unprotected sex with someone, and you are unsure about their sexual history, then an STI screening is recommended.

False. There are many STIs that can be passed on during oral sex, including Chlamydia, Genital Herpes, Gonorrhoea, Hepatitis B and Syphilis.

c. A condom can last between 2 - 5 years after manufacture, if they are looked after, that is, kept away from excessive heat, sunlight and damage from being squashed or torn. Oil-based lubricants, such as massage oil or Vaseline, can damage the latex and increase the risk of the condom breaking. Try to avoid opening the packet with your teeth as you risk tearing. Also watch long nails and jewellery when putting the condom on.

False. A condom should only be used once, carefully withdrawing the penis as soon after ejaculation as possible (holding onto the condom as you go so it doesn't slip of) then removing it, tying the end in a knot, wrapping it and throwing it in the bin (not the toilet – it may cause an embarrassing blockage).

Survival Kit

Do you have more questions about sex?
Visit ☐**www.brook.org.uk**.

Family Planning Sites

Many family planning sites have great question and answer sections and with a bit of searching, you are bound to find the answer to what you are looking for. Be sure to stick to these approved sites, though, otherwise the information you read may not be completely accurate.

SURVIVAL: TEEN ISLAND
The ultimate survival guide for 15 - 18 year olds in Europe.

97

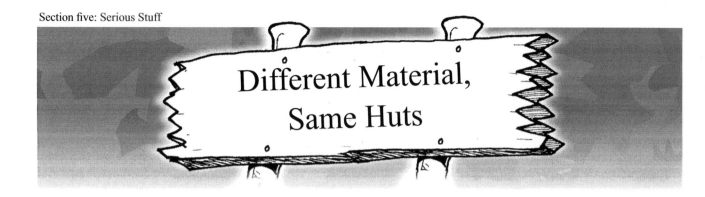

Different Material, Same Huts

In the middle of the ocean, there was an island where a group of people lived in harmony in a happy community. Each family would build a hut made out of palm and they lived their lives in their palm houses. The palm houses looked similar, but each one was a bit different, some were big, some small, some round and some square, but all in all they looked pretty much the same.

One day, one of the islanders left his family, as young men did, and set out to build his hut. But the other islanders were in for a shock. Instead of building his hut out of palm, he used bamboo. In all other ways, the hut had a similar structure to the palm huts, but the way it was built was different. He lived there for a while whilst the other islanders watched and hoped that he would realise how silly he was, and come to his senses and build a palm hut. But he didn't. Pretty soon the islanders got angry. Why was he being so different? At first they just ignored him, then they refused to share their food with him. One night, a group of young islanders got so fed up with him that they stormed his campsite and destroyed his hut. The young man was hurt and confused by this, but undeterred, he built another bamboo hut.

A little while later, another young man decided to build a bamboo hut too. He just decided that he felt better in a hut built out of that material – he never really thought that palm was all that great. He set up a campsite near the first man, who was glad to see that someone felt the same way as him. Over the next few years, a few more men and women joined the bamboo camp. Although it never got as big as the palm camp, it was large enough for the bamboo people to support each other. They were happy amongst themselves, but still a little sad about family and friends from the palm camp that had disowned them.

One night, a massive storm hit the island and completely wiped out the food supply of the palm camp. The people sat around for days, wondering what to do. One young palm camp girl, with green eyes and shiny black hair, said "Why don't we ask the bamboo people for help?" The others reacted with disgust and disbelief, saying "No, we couldn't do that!" "Why not?" the little girl asked.

The palm people went to the old wise man on the hill and asked him if he could explain to the little girl why they could not ask the bamboo people for help. He scratched his head, closed his eyes ... and couldn't come up with an answer.

So the palm people went and asked the bamboo people for help. The bamboo people were a little unsure at first, but they were pretty happy to hear the others talking to them for the first time in ages, so they gave the palm people as much food as they needed. When they were there, the palm people looked around, and for the first time, they didn't see how different the bamboo camp was, but instead they saw that it was pretty much the same as their own.

Years later, the island was a happy, thriving community, where everyone lived together, respecting and celebrating each other's differences. There was an old lady on the island, with green eyes and shiny black hair, said to be the wise one. She used to tell stories to the children about how the island was once divided. Her favourite story was about the little girl who asked "Why not?".

Think about the ways in which this story relates to people that you know who are considered "different".

GAY = **G**OOD **A**S **Y**OU

Bamboo is best

Advice column

What would you write in response to this letter?

I have been best friends with this guy since primary school. We live in the same street. We always used to ride bikes and play footy together but lately he has been pretty quiet.

Some people have started to say that he's gay. He hasn't denied these rumours and when I ask him about it, he doesn't want to talk to me.

I think that everyone may be right and he really is gay.

I don't know what to do about it, though.

Do you have any advice?

Worried - 15.

SURVIVAL: TEEN ISLAND
The ultimate survival guide for 15 - 18 year olds in Europe.

99

Sexuality

If you think you might be gay, lesbian or bisexual:

- Firstly and most importantly, remember that being gay, lesbian or bisexual is normal. It occurs in every country with all different types of people. It just happens to be an orientation that some people find hard to understand and consequently disapprove of it.

- The journey of discovering sexuality and sexual orientation is different for each individual. Being confused for a while is not uncommon and once you have the opportunity to talk to others in similar situations, you will find that they might have had similar times of confusion.

- There is no one reason why people are gay. Some try to consider the genetic and social influences, but this can be confusing – it's easier just to realise that some people are gay and some are straight just like some people have blue eyes, not brown. There are natural variations in all characteristics of humans. It's just the way things are and it makes our world a rich and interesting place to be.

- Just because a person has some feelings of attraction or admiration towards a person of the same sex, it does not necessarily mean that they are gay. There are many forms and degrees of attraction. Perhaps it might help to think of attraction on a scale with men at one end and women at the other, and people can fall at any point on the scale or move along it during different stages in their lives.

- Some gay, lesbian or bisexual people say that they have always known about their sexuality or "felt different" from their peers, whilst others do not discover their feelings until adolescence or even later in adulthood.

- Over time, people will usually be able to work out whether they are attracted to males or females or both. This may involve experiences with one gender or both. It will usually be easier for a person to come to the right conclusions for them if they have the support of family and friends, and/or have access to community support services.

- Some people will probably find it easier to "come out" than others. Some will feel comfortable telling most people that they meet. Others may only be comfortable letting close friends or family know.

If you feel like you want to tell people about your sexuality, keep these points in mind:

- It might be helpful to tell one person at a time, starting with someone that you trust and think will be most accepting. This person can then support you in telling others. If you don't have someone like this, make sure you know of a support service that can help you in this process.

- If you are feeling unhappy or guilty about your sexuality, it might not be the best time to tell anyone that you think might react badly – they may make you feel worse. Wait until you are more comfortable about your situation so you can tell these people with confidence and self-assurance.

- It might help to get your hands on a good book or pamphlet that can provide family and friends with some answers to their questions. If anyone reacts badly, giving them this material might help them to process their thoughts and understand your situation better.

- If you are dependent on someone that you think may react badly, it might be an idea to wait for a time that you can support yourself, or have a back-up plan of a trusted friend or relative that you can stay with.

- Expose people to the concept of being gay first – for example watch a television show with them that features a gay character and casually converse about the character to "suss out" the feelings of those close to you. If your family and friends react positively and openly about these characters, this can be (not always, but usually) a good sign.

- The idea that you will never "get married" may seem upsetting or daunting, but many gay people settle down with a life partner, just like straight people do. Already, laws are changing to give same-sex couples the same rights as straight couples. It is now possible to have a same-sex relationship legally recognised with a civil partnership, in many countries.

SURVIVAL: TEEN ISLAND
The ultimate survival guide for 15 - 18 year olds in Europe.

101

☐ If you are having concerns about your own sexuality, there are plenty of support agencies which will be able to listen to your experiences and give advice on coming out, dealing with harassment and discrimination, and finding ways of exploring your feelings in a way that is the safest for you, physically and emotionally. There is also plenty of information on safe sex, relevant to your situation.

☐ Good news! Every day, the world is becoming more gay-friendly. Even in the last five years, there have been changes in the law that have supported the rights of gay people and positive media and television exposure which has portrayed gay and lesbian people in positive ways.

Some religions condemn homosexuality, but the fact is there have always been and will always be gay people in the world.

Gay Friend?

If you think someone you know
might be gay, lesbian or bisexual:

☐ Don't ask them "point blank" – you might be completely off track and they may take offence, or you might be right, but they are still trying to sort it out within themselves. Wait for them to tell you. If you want to be helpful, then perhaps find ways of showing them that you are a trustworthy and accepting friend.

☐ If they are a good friend, do not disown them – this has the potential to damage their self-esteem and self-worth and make them afraid to tell others. Remember they are the same person they have always been – telling you about their sexual orientation does not change the person that they are.

☐ What you see on television is only a small representation of what gay people are like. You can't always tell if a person is gay just by talking to them – avoid thinking in stereotypes.

☐ Not everyone will be comfortable with "labels". Some people may engage in same-sex relationships but may not call themselves "gay" or "lesbian". This is fine, as it is up to the individual and how they think of themselves.

☐ If you know someone who has told you that they are gay, or who you think might be gay, then remember that the most important things are to listen and to not be judgemental about that person. Instead of bombarding them with personal questions that they may not feel comfortable about answering, just allow them to talk. Focus on their feelings before expressing yours. This is an important, and probably difficult, thing for them to be doing.

☐ A common misconception: Just because your friend is gay, it does not necessarily mean that they are sexually attracted to you, or everyone of the same sex. Telling you about their sexuality may in fact be one of the hardest things they have ever had to do and chances are they just want your acceptance and support.

Same-Sex Survival Kit

The websites below might be helpful if you have questions about sexuality. The benefit of browsing the web is that it is confidential, you can do it at your own pace, and there will be a variety of information from which you can take what you need. Be careful, though, not everything out there will send true or positive messages. If you are unsure, check the facts across a couple of sources – if the information is consistent, it is more likely to be of benefit to you. Your area may have a gay and lesbian newspaper that will tell you about what's on and how to access support and social groups.

International Lesbian and gay association http://www.ilga-europe.org/

Lesbian, Gay, Bisexual and Transgender Rights

http://www.tuc.org.uk/equality/index.cfm?mins=21&minors=21

Dazz-Elle New Drug & Alcohol Website for Young Lesbians http://www.dazz-elle.org.uk/

Gaybourhood http://www.gingerbeer.co.uk

Beau Belles http://www.myspace.com/beaubelles

BeYou http://www.beyou.org.uk/ Be You Helpline 0118 959 7269

Bisexual Underground (The) http://www.bisexualunderground.org/

Broken Rainbow Broken Rainbow LGBT Domestic Violence Helpline provides support to LGBT people, family, and friends experiencing domestic violence. Our national helpline service is confidential and staffed by LGBT persons. 08452 60 44 60

Bulgayria bulgayria is a web site about the news on gay/lesbian/ homosexual/queer life in Bulgaria http://www.gay.bg/

Connections North London Haringey: 07841 986 226 Enfield: 07841 986 229

Gaire http://www.gaire.com/ Gay info for Ireland.

Herts Gay Community http://www.gayherts.org.uk

Octopus http://www.octopusgroup.org.uk/ OCTOPUS is a local gay social group based around the east side of London and the Essex borders.

The Blackdown Social Group is a social group for gay men in Devon, South & West Somerset and West Dorset. http:// blackdownsocialgroup.org.uk/

SURVIVAL: TEEN ISLAND
The ultimate survival guide for 15 - 18 year olds in Europe.

103

The Event of the Year

For one night of the year, amidst all the trials and tribulations of surviving on your island, all of the stresses are magically removed as a dazzling luxury cruise ship picks you up and takes you out for an evening of glamour. Your fellow islanders transform into sophisticated stars, the red carpet is rolled out and you feel like royalty as you dine on fine foods and dance the night away. That's right, it's the school ball – the night of nights on your social calendar.

But who would believe that leading up to this exclusive event was a series of stresses about dresses, make-up mayhem, tux mix-ups, and corsage chaos? As girls go into grief mode about colour clashes and guys pierce their nipples whilst pinning flowers to their suits, the parents sit back and wonder what all the fuss is about, as they see their teen's life savings get stashed into the pockets of one greasy limo driver.

Is there a way to look nifty but be thrifty?
To look flash but save cash?
Read on, penny-pinchers!

Gals:

(Guilt-free glamour)

- Check out second-hand boutiques (some just specialise in designer wear and formal gowns), hire shops and the newspaper classifieds section for dresses. If you don't tell anyone, it is unlikely that they will even know, and you will be slashing the price. You may also have the luck to be in a time or place where "vintage" is in.

- Try your (or your mum's) hand at sewing. You will get the perfect dress, in the right colour, fitting perfectly.

- Do your own make-up. So many girls get a makeover done, which costs money, takes a long time and often ends up looking hideous as some make-up artists do not understand the concept of "less is more". You may be able to invest in some nice new make-up for a fraction of the cost, plus you get to keep it. Some girls may go for getting their brows shaped or eyelashes tinted – this again may be cheaper but lasts longer. Sisters, cousins and cool next door neighbours are also an invaluable resource here.

- Have a "beauty spa treatment day" at home with your friends. Ask each person to bring a few ingredients and enjoy a pamper session for under £10. Go one step further and each bring one good quality cosmetic and help each other do make-up.

- If you do get your hair done, simple is often better, will cost less and take less time. Make sure you allow plenty of time for getting your hair done. Some hairdressers who are still training may do your hair for a reduced cost, and since they are learning, they may actually try even harder to make it look better.

- Fragrance samples from department stores are perfect for one night of yummy scent.

- Go for bargain jewellery, not real diamonds and gold – chances are you will only wear it once.

- Use gowns worn by stars at the Oscars as inspiration for home-made dresses.

- Find a girlfriend or cousin who goes to another school and split the cost of one, super-special dress.

- Buy some ordinary shoes and then use a hot glue gun to add some sequins or another special touch.

- With your parents, decide on an overall budget. That way, if you save money in one area, e.g. by growing your nails instead of getting fake ones, you are allowed to splurge a little on another area.

- Throughout the year, save vouchers for hair, make-up, etc. to use on the big day.

Hot Tips for The School Ball

DO NOT USE hairsprays or any aerosol in a confined space. Make sure the area is ventilated and make sure there are no heat sources. Vapour from aerosols lingers in a confined space and can explode on contact with a heat source, causing burns and even death.

3 Weeks to go!!!!

SURVIVAL: TEEN ISLAND
The ultimate survival guide for 15 - 18 year olds in Europe.

105

Guys

☐ Guys, how about raiding grandma's garden for a home-made corsage or just give your gal a bunch of flowers. The thought will count.

☐ It's not just tuxes – funky suits are now quite acceptable to wear at balls. Check with your cousins or even your dad to see if they have anything you can try on. Best of all, you don't need to get up at the crack of dawn to return it to the hire shop the next day!

Both

☐ Organise as much fundraising at your school as possible so that you save on the cost of the ticket.

☐ Take heaps of photos before you go and maybe only order one or two of the ones offered by the school.

☐ Host pre-ball drinks with mock-tails. It has the cool effect but you won't turn up to the ball looking like a wasted wreck.

☐ Do you really need a limo? What about a taxi – it gives you the same amount of independence with a heap more cash to spare.

☐ Talk to your teachers about banning newspaper photographers and competitions such as "Belle of the Ball". These are only bound to select out a few and cause rivalry.

☐ Buy your shoes a few weeks beforehand and wear them in around the house – your feet will thank you.

☐ Take some money with you for emergencies.

Source: ☐http://articles.findarticles.
com/p/articles/mi_m0NAH/is_5_32/ai_87854531

SURVIVAL: TEEN ISLAND
The ultimate survival guide for 15 - 18 year olds in Europe.

The Invasion

So there you are, enjoying your idyllic little piece of paradise, basking in the peaceful sunlight, looking out on the horizon at the lapping waves, the playful dolphins and the ferry full of happy tourists ... make that happy, noisy tourists ... um, make that excited, rowdy tourists ... quite young, in big groups ... where are their parents? Suddenly, the realisation dawns upon you. It's holiday clubbing week! Batten down the hatches and prepare for the storm!

Holiday clubbing week has become somewhat of a rite of passage for school leavers throughout Europe who are ready to let their hair down and celebrate after months of hard work and study. Many students take this opportunity to travel with their friends to various holiday destinations throughout the country, and for many, it's the first time they have ever been away without their parents.

It is important for young people to remember that it is a privilege that their parents are trusting them and allowing this opportunity. There are a few ways to repay this trust and ensure that holiday clubbing week is an adventure, not a disaster.

SURVIVAL: TEEN ISLAND
The ultimate survival guide for 15 - 18 year olds .

107

Clubbing Holidays

You have made it! The final exams are just about over and you are ready to jump head first into party time. But take a little time out to plan your well-earned rest.

Just by taking a few precautions, you can enjoy your time a lot more. Most of these are common sense, and pretty subtle – you don't need to look like a geek to be aware of the risks.

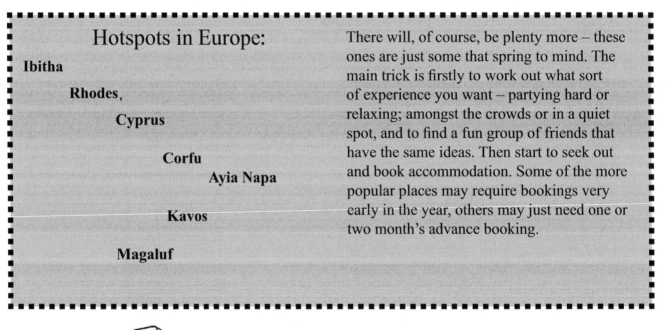

Hotspots in Europe:

Ibitha

  Rhodes,

    Cyprus

      Corfu

        Ayia Napa

      Kavos

  Magaluf

There will, of course, be plenty more – these ones are just some that spring to mind. The main trick is firstly to work out what sort of experience you want – partying hard or relaxing; amongst the crowds or in a quiet spot, and to find a fun group of friends that have the same ideas. Then start to seek out and book accommodation. Some of the more popular places may require bookings very early in the year, others may just need one or two month's advance booking.

108

SURVIVAL: TEEN ISLAND
The ultimate survival guide for 15 - 18 year olds in Europe.

☐ Contact local tourist bureaus, make use of travel agents or jump on the net to find out more about where you want to stay. Other aspects to bear in mind include cost, how to get there and get around, things to do, what the weather will be like and so on.

☐ see http://www.ibiza-spotlight.com for hints and tips on how to survive an Ibiza clubbing holiday. NB: you must be 18 to enter the clubs in Ibiza.

see http://www.dearcupid.org/ for relationship advice

Directory of party clubbing and nightclub

geared holidays http://www.travel-quest. co.uk/tqdance.htm

Clubbing abroad http://www. clubbingabroad.co.uk/bookmarks/

The Student Room http://www. thestudentroom.co.uk

Real holiday reports http://www. realholidayreports.com

Orange smile http://www.orangesmile.com

Accommodation Advice:

☒ Work out costs for accommodation and food before you go so that you avoid conflict within your group.

☐ Get a copy of the rules when you are booking a place and if they seem unfair or you think they will be difficult to abide by, then book somewhere else. Check for any "hidden costs" and make sure that the rates are reasonable. Not all places charge a security bond, however if you have one, make sure of the conditions under which it will be refunded. If you have any concerns, call the Office of Fair Trading. (Check your White Pages® for local numbers.)

☐ When you check in to the accommodation, check for any damage and inform the manager straight away in writing so your group is not blamed for it.

☐ Take care with valuables in your room – it might be useful to check with the manager about safe facilities at your accommodation. Leave expensive jewellery and clothing at home.

☐ Pack some warm clothes – often nights will be cool and many places may have beach parties or similar where you will be outdoors at night.

☐ Pack a first aid kit for your accommodation. Always have some water in your room.

☐ Decide about food before you leave. If your accommodation has kitchen facilities, it might be helpful to take staples such as tinned food, pasta, rice, etc. from home. It will be cheaper and easier and you won't have to worry about so much shopping when you are there.

SURVIVAL: TEEN ISLAND
The ultimate survival guide for 15 - 18 year olds in Europe.

109

House Rules:

- ☐ Talk to your mates about some "house rules" at the start.

- ☐ Remember that underage drinking or using fake ID is illegal and can cop you a huge fine.

- ☐ Don't forget that the places that you are invading are also people's homes. Respect the locals by limiting litter, noise and reckless behaviour. You wouldn't want it to be happening in your back yard.

Before You Go Out:

- ☐ Drink water and eat some decent food before a big night out.

- ☐ Before you go out, plan how you are getting home. Also have a meeting point if you become separated and use text messages (with vibration) to let friends know where you are.

Partying Supplies:

- ☐ Take a mobile phone and put all important numbers in it (including your family, the friends you are with and local public transport and taxi numbers) before you go. Make sure it is charged up and cashed up.

- ☐ Make sure you always have between £20 and £50 cash with you for emergency taxis.

- ☐ Take public transport timetables with you and make sure you are aware of times and the location of major stations.

- ☐ Take water with you. This will prevent dehydration and by carrying your own water, you reduce the risk of taking spiked drinks from strangers. You can get water bottle holders with a strap that can hang over your neck.

- ☐ Make sure you have ID on you. Also a European Health Insurance card will help in an emergency situation, (DO NOT LEAVE THE UK WITHOUT ONE) The card entitles the holder to free or reduced-cost healthcare in Europe but has an expiry date, **SO CHECK YOURS** and you should know private health and/or travel insurance cover details, if you have them.

- ☐ Pockets are better then a huge, obvious purse. Travel smart but travel light.

- ☐ If there is any chance that you or one of your friends may be sexually active, take some condoms, rwhether you are a boy or a girl. It will protect from pregnancy and STDs and even if you don't end up using them yourself, one of your friends may thank you. Remember if you are on the pill and you have thrown up at any stage, this can make the pill ineffective.

SURVIVAL: TEEN ISLAND
The ultimate survival guide for 15 - 18 year olds in Europe.

☐ Wear a watch so you can be more prepared for meet up times.

☐ Wear sensible, closed in shoes to avoid being stomped on or cutting your feet with glass.

☐ Wear a hat and sunscreen during the day, otherwise you will be suffering and miss out on the celebrations in the evening.

Watch Out:

☐ If you are intimate with someone, especially a person you do not know very well, listen to them very carefully. If they say "No!" stop immediately. If you don't, you may be committing an act of forced sexual behaviour, which is a crime.

☐ Sexual assault is a reality – for females and males. Be very wary of anyone who makes you feel uncomfortable or tries to get you alone. Remain in a busy area and preferably amongst friends.

☐ There are many people who are there to help. The police are just doing their job and are the best people to approach if you feel that you are in any kind of danger or just need a bit of help, advice or support. Many locations also have young people volunteering to assist.

☐ If you think your drink has been spiked, ask for help and seek an ambulance, or get to a hospital ASAP. The best two defences are not letting your drink, or your friends that you trust, out of your sight.

☐ If you think your friend or someone nearby is reacting badly to something they have consumed, call an ambulance. The ambulance officer is there to look after the patient.

☐ Be super-aware of lecherous people, particularly older adults who like to prey on drunk young teenagers. Non-school leavers who go to hotspots can be dodgy. Avoid places like dark rooms, alleyways, sand dunes and quiet streets. If you feel you are being watched or followed, go to a public place where there are lots of people and tell a police officer if you see such a person.

☐ Prepare for things such as break-ups, fallouts with friends, or annoying friends doing drugs or bringing strangers back to accommodation.

☐ Never leave a friend alone if they have passed out. They may choke on their own vomit. Make sure they are on their side and have a clear airway.

> **Remember**
>
> # 999 or 112
>
> **for all emergencies.**
>
> **If you have any major concerns and cannot get any other help, call Children in Crisis**
>
> # 020 7627 1040
>
> **or**
>
> **Childline (free call)**
>
> # 0800 1111

SURVIVAL: TEEN ISLAND
The ultimate survival guide for 15 - 18 year olds in Europe.

111

MORE HELP

GENERAL

Go to http://**www.childline.org.uk** for help on anything.

Bullying Problems at school, college or work

www.bullybusters.org.uk 0800 1696928

Shadow CS www.shadiowcs.co.uk. This is a fun website aimed at young people up to the age of 16 and is about crime. It allows young people to get involved in discussions about crime and the everyday things that affcet you as a young person.

Teenage Health Freak http://www.teenagehealthfreak.org/ has great advice and information that all young people need to know.

After Adoption http://www.afteradoption.org.uk 0800 0 568 578

DIVORCE/REMARRIAGE OF PARENTS:

- □www.cyh.com contains information for youth on a variety of topics, including family breakdowns.

DEATH OF FAMILY MEMBER:

If someone you love has died each of these sites can help.

The Cruse Bereavement Centre http://www.rd4u.org.uk FREE phone helpline: 0808 808 1677 (Monday - Friday, 9:30 am - 5:00 pm)

Winston's Wish http://www.winstonswish.org.uk Helpline telephone 08452 03 04 05

The Child Bereavement Charity http://www.childbereavement.org.uk 01494 446648

Support Line http://www.supportline.org.uk This is confidential support (that means they can't tell anyone like your mum or dad) 020 8554 9004

Baby Loss www.babyloss.com * Babyloss, PO Box 1168, Southampto SO15 8XZ, UK or email support@babyloss.com

General well-being & advice

Lifebytes www.lifebytes.gov.uk

Mind, Body & Soul www.mindbodysoul.gov.uk

NSPCC www.worriedneed2talk.org.uk

Connexions www.connexions-direct.com

Youth Access www.youthaccess.org.uk

Help4kids (Northern Ireland) www.help4kids.co.uk

HEALTH

NHS WWW.NHSDIRECT.ORG.UK

LIFE BYTES HTTP://WWW.LIFEBYTES GOV.UK

MINDY BODY AND SOUL WWW.MINDBODYSOUL.GOV.UK

HEADS AWAY JUST SAY WWW.HEADS-AWAY-JUST-SAY.COM

TRUST ERIC WWW.TRUSTERIC.ORG

MENINGITIS TRUST /WWW MENINGITIS-TRUST.ORG/

ASTHMA WWW.ASTHMA.ORG.UK

TALK4TEENS WWW.TALK4TEENS.CO.UK

5 A DAY
WWW.5ADAY.NHS.UK

WILLOW FOUNDATION
WWW.WILLOWFOUNDATION.ORG.UK

NETDOCTOR WWW.NETDOCTOR.CO.UK/

SUICIDE OF FAMILY MEMBER:

Better Health Channel http://www.betterhealth.vic.gov.au/bhcv2/bhcarticles.nsf/pages/Suicide_family_and_friends?OpenDocument

Kids Health www.kidshealth.org/

MENTAL ILLNESS:

NHS CHOICES YOUR HEALTH, YOUR CHOICES

WWW.NHS.UK/LIVEWELL/PAGES/LIVEWELLHUB.ASPX

DRUGS AND ALCOHOL:

National Association for children of alcoholics 08003583456

http://kidshealth.com/teen/drug_alcohol/

EATING DISORDERS:

www.naturallyhealthylifestyles.com

www.answerbag.co.uk/

www.eatingdisorderinteen.com

SEXUAL HEALTH/PREGNANCY/ABORTION:

Rape Crisis England and Wales. http://www.rapecrisis.org.uk, if you or someone you know has been the victim of sexual violence then they can help

Remember the vast majority of young people are decent hard working people. There is no law that says you must have sex with someone. There is no law that says you must take a drug or abuse alcohol. There is nothing wrong with being a young person who, for the moment, does not feel totally comfortable yet in having a sexual relationship. There is nothing wrong in waiting for Mr or Miss Right. *There is nothing wrong in being you*.

SURVIVAL: TEEN ISLAND
The ultimate survival guide for 15 - 18 year olds in Europe.

113

• **Victim Supportline** Call 0845 30 30 900
Victim Support is the independent national charity which helps people cope with crime. We have a network of local branches across England, Wales and Northern Ireland. There are separate organisations covering Scotland and the Republic of Ireland.

Mankind UK is a UK charity that offers support and advice on surviving man sexual abuse, sexual attack or sexual assault.

Telephone : 01273 510447 Mankind UK

P.O.Box 124, Newhaven,, East Sussex

BN9 9TQ

Counselling directory www.counselling-directory.org.uk/ this website is a support network of UK counsellors and psychotherapists, with information on their training and experience, areas of counselling covered, fees and contact details. This service is free, confidential and easy to use.

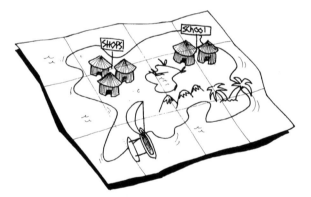

Rape crisis England and Wales www.rapecrisis.org.uk/ This website aims to provide the basic information that survivors of sexual violence, friends and family need to access the services they need.

http://www.rapecrisis.org.uk/members.html This page gives you details of UK wode services.

Rape crisis Scotland 08088 010302
WWW.RAPECRISISSCOTLAND.ORG.UK/

RAPE CRISIS NETWORK IRELAND
WWW.RCNI.IE/ 1800778888

RAPE CRISIS NETWORK EUROPE ,

RAPE CRISIS NETWORK IRELAND, THE

HALLS, QUAY ST, GALWAY, IRELAND.,

TEL: +353 91 563 676

FAX: +353 91 563 677

EMAIL: RCNI@EIRCOM.NET

DOMESTIC VIOLENCE:
(these services are mainly aimed at women)

Women's aid http://www.womensaid.org.uk/
08082000247

Family onwards: www.familyonwards.com

Refuge for women and children against domestic violence 0808 2000 247Freephone 24-hour National Domestic Violence Helpline (run in partnership between Women's Aid and Refuge)

CAB advice Guide /www.adviceguide.org.uk

Women's domestic violence helpline
0161 636 7525 there is a facility on the site to hide your visit so no-one can trace you were there. Remember that someone else may have access to your telephone bills that may be itemised. If you don't want people at home to know you have rung the Helpline, ring from a friend's house or a phone box

•

HOMELESSNESS/POVERTY:

The Salvation Army is one organisation which provides assistance and emergency accommodation for homeless youth or young people in other crisis situations. Go to www.salvationarmy.org.uk/or look up local Salvation Army services in your local telephone directory.

Shelter Cymru http://www.sheltercymru.org.uk/shelter/home/

Shelter England http://england.shelter.org.uk/get_advice/advice_topics/homelessness

Shelter Scotland http://scotland.shelter.org.uk/getadvice

DISABILITY:

If someone in your family, such as a parent or sibling, has a disability:

- **Mencap** www.mencap.org.uk/

- **Check the map** www.checkthemap.org/: this is a database of learning disability services.

Special needs and disability Services / www.britishservices.co.uk/disabilities.htm

ADOPTION:

ADOPTION INFORMATION LINE WWW.ADOPTION.ORG.UK

BRITISH ASSOCIATION FOR ADOPTING AND FOSTERING WWW.BAAF.ORG.UK/

WWW.ADOPTIONMATCH.CO.UK/

REMEMBER, you are NEVER ALONE.

You can always get help, no matter what the problem is. Using one of the help support schemes here is a sign of STRENGTH NOT WEAKNESS

see
www.aber-publishing.co.uk
www.studymates.co.uk
for more information

SURVIVAL: TEEN ISLAND
The ultimate survival guide for 15 - 18 year olds in Europe.

115